MENSA
— Publications —

THE ULTIMATE
MENTAL
CHALLENGE

THIS IS A CARLTON BOOK

Text copyright © British Mensa Limited 1995
Design and artwork copyright © Carlton Books Limited

This edition published by Carlton Books Limited 1996

A CIP catalogue for this book is available from the British Library

ISBN 1-85868-116-2

Designed by Jacqui Sheard

Printed in Great Britain

MENSA
— Publications —

THE ULTIMATE
MENTAL
CHALLENGE

Robert Allen

CARLTON

CONTENTS

You might think it silly to call a puzzle book *The Ultimate Mental Challenge*. After all, it's only a bit of fun, isn't it? Surely a grandiose title like that should be reserved for something serious and worthy, the sort of mental effort associated with Einstein or Beethoven or Shakespeare. But wait! These puzzles may be of no importance whatever. It doesn't really matter whether you can solve them or not – except to you. Just let yourself get hooked on this book (the easy section is simply there to lure you in), and you will find the challenge irresistible. A curious relationship exists between a puzzle setter and the reader. Each tries to read the other's mind, to anticipate the mental processes that go into the construction of a puzzle. It becomes a battle of wits in which either side strives for supremacy. So although you may not think this is your ultimate challenge, you could be in for a surprise.

If you like puzzles you will like Mensa, a society that exists entirely for people who are adept at solving the knottiest problems. If you would like to take the Mensa test and meet people of like mind, then write to us at British Mensa Limited, Mensa House, St John's Square, Wolverhampton, WV2 4AH England.

I should like to thank all those who helped with this book. In particular I should like to mention my wife Doris, our friend Josie Fulton, and puzzler David Ballheimer, who edits my outpourings without mercy and saves me from making a fool of myself in public.

R. P. Allen

ROBERT ALLEN
Editorial Director, Mensa Publications
June, 1995

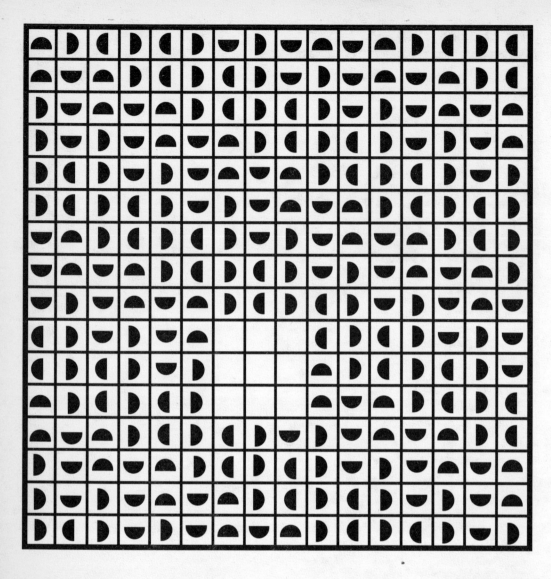

PUZZLE 1

Which of these patterns fits into the blank section?

See answer **25**

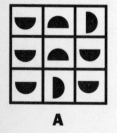

A

B

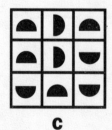

C

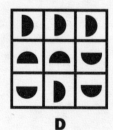

D

2 3 5 8 13 21 34 ?

PUZZLE 2

Can you find the number which comes next in this sequence?

See answer **81**

PUZZLE 3

Can you correct this equation by moving one match?

See answer **28**

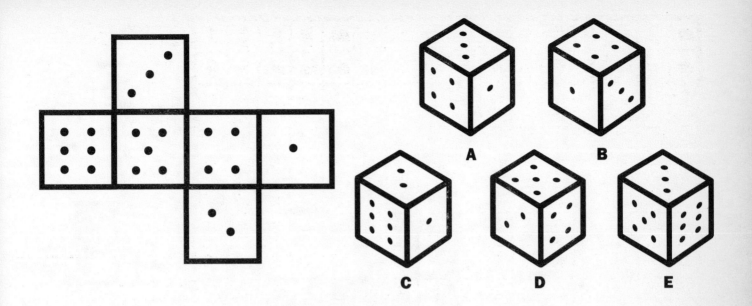

PUZZLE 4

Which of the following cubes cannot be
made from this layout?

See answer 15

I have five hands but you would pass me in the street without comment.

Why?

PUZZLE 5

See answer 46

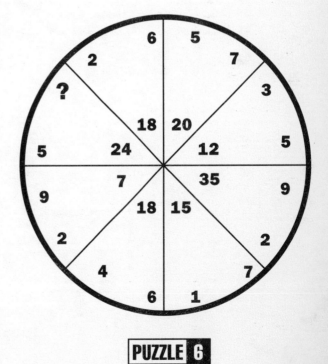

PUZZLE 6

Can you replace the question mark
with a number to meet
the conditions of the wheel?

See answer 58

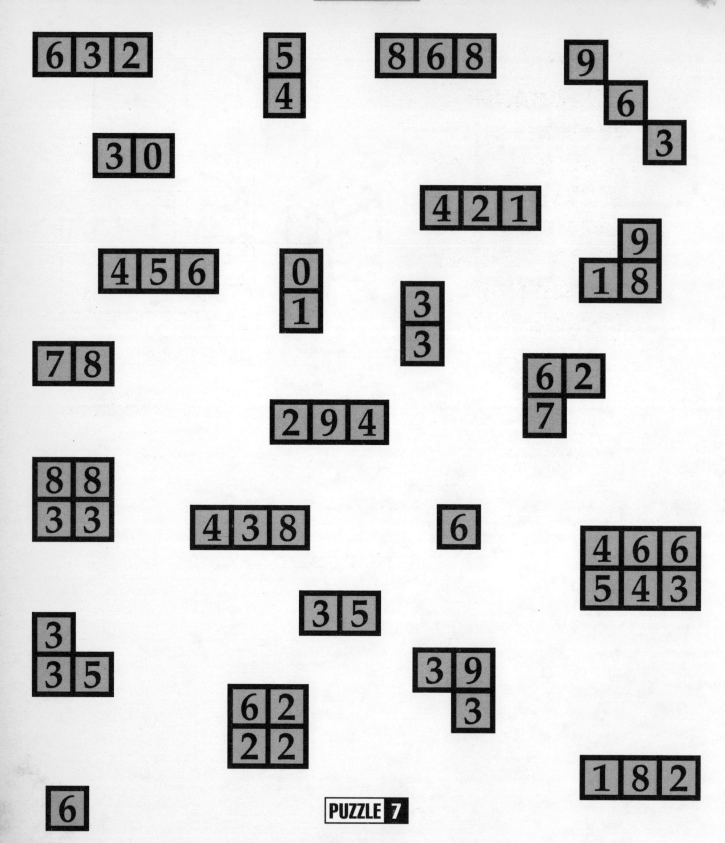

PUZZLE 7

These tiles, when placed in right order, will form
a square in which each horizontal line is
identical with one vertical line.
Can you successfully form the square?

See answer 33

PUZZLE 8

ULFCHANIH
VYNBYMXU
WIFOGVCU JCEY
MCFPYL MJLCHA
GIOHN LUCHCYL
WBYPS WBUMY
AYILAYNIQH
UHUWIMNCU

Here are the coded names of some places in or
around Washington, D.C. Try to unravel them.

See answer 62

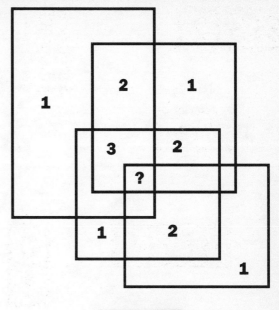

PUZZLE 9

This diagram was constructed according to a certain
logic. Can you work out which number should
replace the question mark?

See answer 104

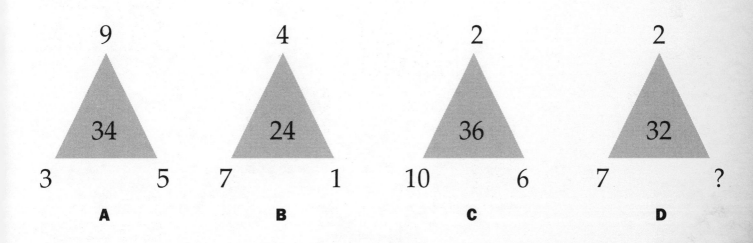

PUZZLE 10

Can you find the number to go at the bottom of
triangle D?

See answer 87

PUZZLE 11

Can you find the letter which completes
the diagram?

See answer 22

PUZZLE 12

Can you find out the relationship of the letters and
numbers in this square and find out which number
should replace the question mark?

See answer 35

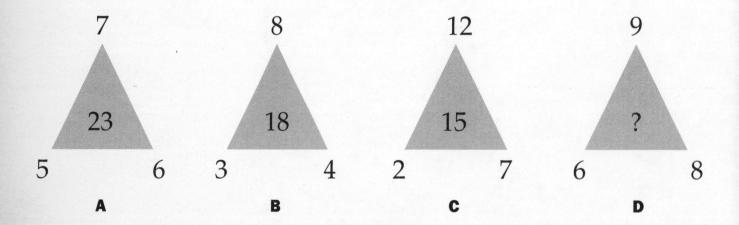

PUZZLE 13

Can you work out how the numbers in the triangles
are related and find the missing number?

See answer 39

To celebrate her sixth birthday, Samantha planted a tree in her parents' garden.

She had often watched her dad plant things and she did it just right.

She even remembered to water it in.

Her mother was furious. She said that the tree belonged to her and Samantha had no business planting it.

However, her father thought it was funny but explained to her that the tree would never grow.

Why?

See answer 41

VKHEOHC   (Russian)

THRBCE   (German)

EWDIL   (Irish)

TBTEEKC   (Irish)

TGNEE   (French)

EEOHTG   (German)

NBESI   (Norwegian)

CAIREN   (French)

PUZZLE 15

The above are all anagrams of the names of famous playrights. The nationality is given in brackets to help you.

See answer 114

PUZZLE 16

Can you find the odd ball out?

See answer 122

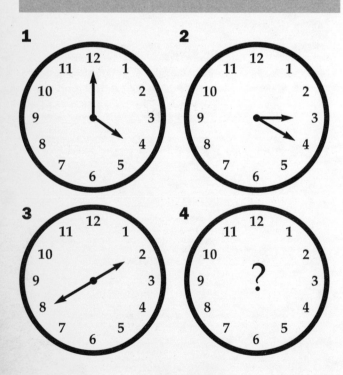

PUZZLE 17

Can you work out the time on the blank clock face?

See answer 83

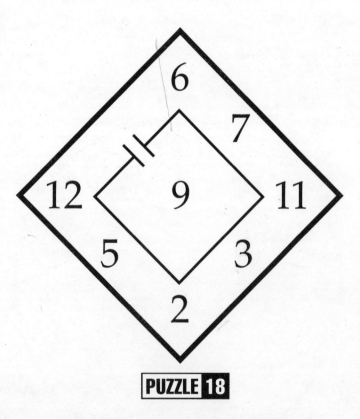

PUZZLE 18

In this diagram, starting from the top of the diamond and working in a clockwise direction, the four basic mathematical signs (+, −, x, ÷) have been omitted. Your task is to restore them so that the calculation, with answer in the middle, is correct.

See answer 6

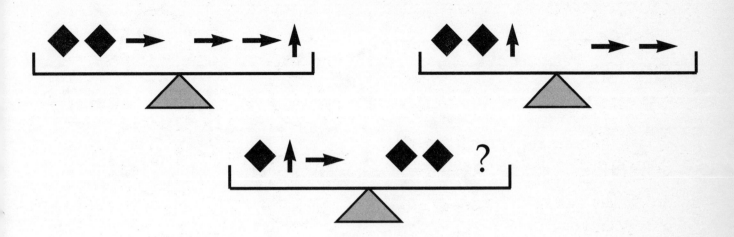

PUZZLE 19

Can you find the symbol that will balance the
last set of scales?

See answer 101

PUZZLE 20

The diagram represents an old-fashioned telephone
dial with letters as well as numbers. Below is a list of
numbers representing ten American States. Can you
use the diagram to decode them?

See answer 1

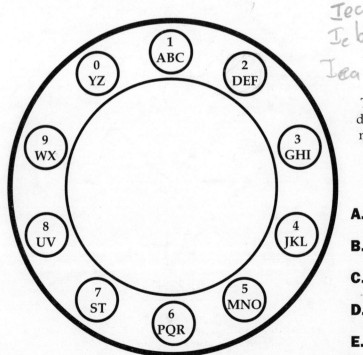

A.	1143256531	F.	562355
B.	72917	G.	83633531
C.	52161741	H.	2456321
D.	141741	I.	15456125
E.	32135	J.	1630551

handwritten answers: A. CALIFORNIA, B. Texas, C. NEBRASKA, D. Alaska, E. IDAHO, F. Oregon, G. Virginia, H. Florida, I. Colorado, J. Arizona

A   **is to**   **B**   **as**   **C**   **is to**

D   **E**

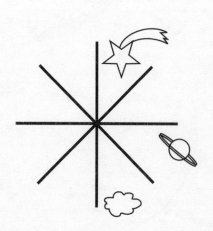

F   **G**

PUZZLE 21

See answer **127**

16

PUZZLE 22

Can you find the odd face out?

See answer 12

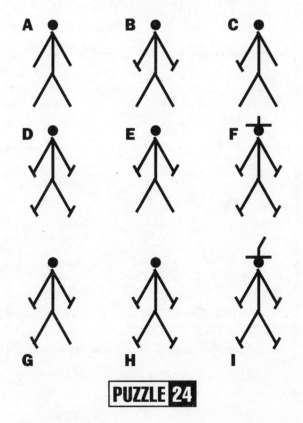

PUZZLE 24

Which matchstick man, G, H or L, would carry on the sequence?

See answer 49

YVRKYIFN
WFIK NFIKY
SVE XLIZFE
CRJ GRCDRJ
F'YRIV
XRKNZTB
YREVUR
JYREEFE

PUZZLE 23

The above is a simple substitution code which conceals the names of eight international airports. See if you can crack the code.

See answer 128

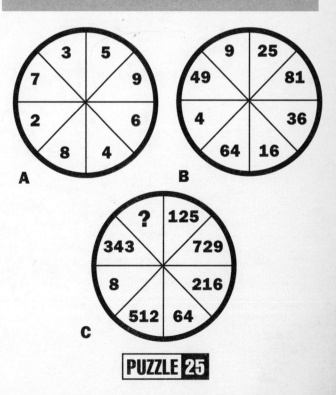

PUZZLE 25

A curious logic governs the numbers in these circles. Can you discover what it is and then work out what the missing number should be?

See answer 9

PUZZLE 26

These tiles, when placed in right order, will form
a square in which each horizontal line is
identical with one vertical line.
Can you successfully form the square?

See answer **51**

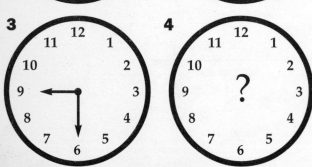

PUZZLE 27

The above clocks move in a certain pattern.
Can you work out the time on the last clock?

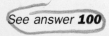
See answer **100**

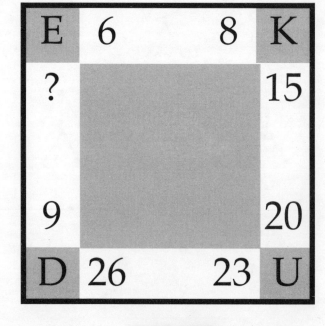

PUZZLE 28

The letters and numbers in this square follow
a pattern. Can you work out which number
represents the question mark?

See answer **19**

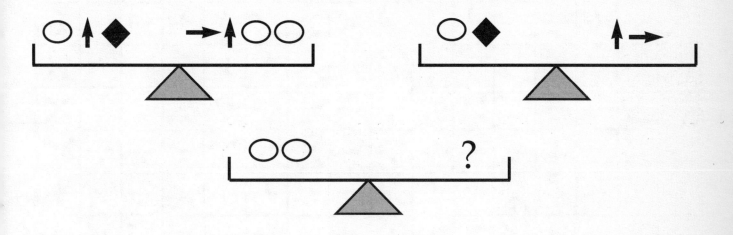

PUZZLE 29

Can you find out which symbol would
balance the third scale?

See answer 96

2
5
9
14
20
?

PUZZLE 30

Can you complete this series?

See answer 106

A C C O H G I
W L K E E M U I A
U T S O O N H
G N H I A M M R B I
R T O E I D T
A A A T T N L
X P E H O I N
P M H E I M S

PUZZLE 31

The above are all anagrams of the names of American
cities. Can you work out which they are?

See answer 105

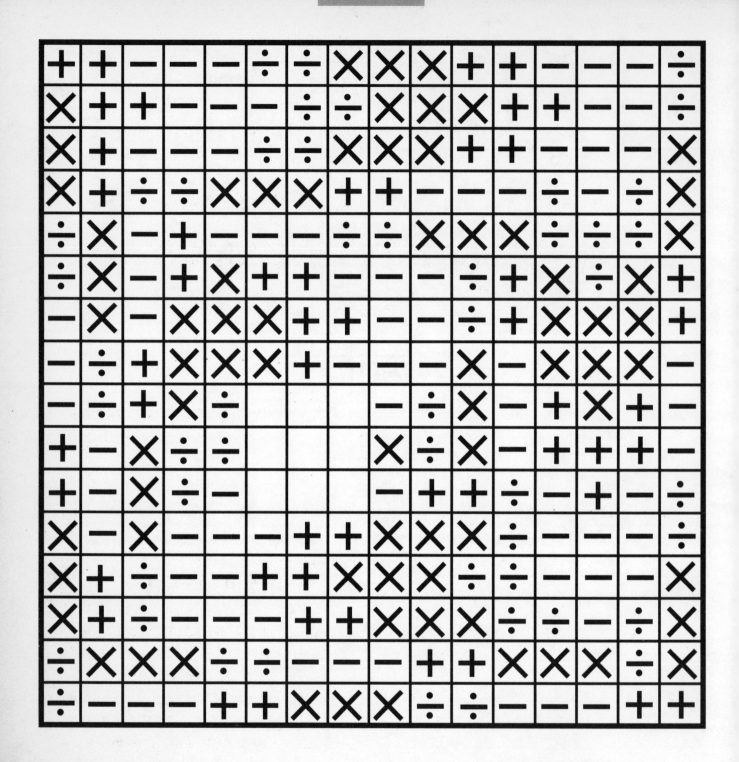

PUZZLE 32

A section of this grid has been removed and its symbols deleted. Can you replace the symbols so that the logic of the grid is restored?

See answer 27

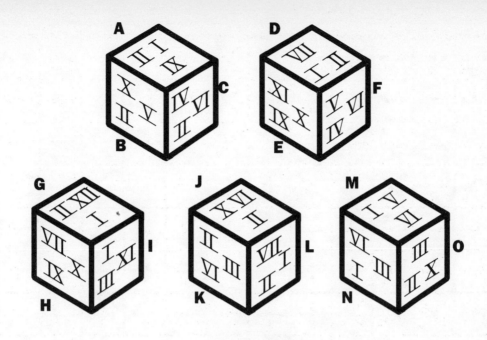

PUZZLE 33

Can you work out which two sides on these cubes
have identical numbers?

See answer 130

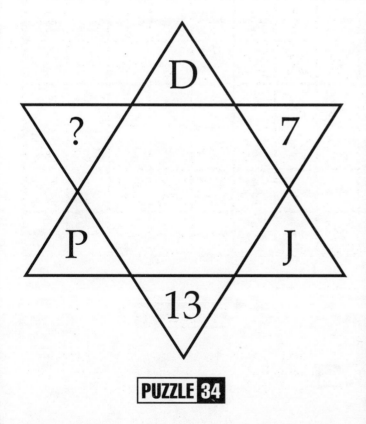

PUZZLE 34

Can you find the number to complete the diagram?

See answer 21

```
          7 1 26 16 1 3 8 15
    13 21 12 12 9 7 1 20 1 23 14 25
          2 15 18 19 3 8 20
       13 9 14 5 19 20 18 15 14 5
           3 8 15 23 4 5 18
      1 22 7 15 12 5 13 15 14 15
        3 15 3 11-1-12 5 5 11 9 5
      2 15 21 9 12 12 1 2 1 9 19 19 5
```

PUZZLE 35

The above is a substitution code which
uses numbers in place of letters. The words that
have been encoded are all types of soup
from around the world.

See answer 119

E O G O N R
A R B S E N A K
A V D N E A
C I S N O W N I S
R I O D A L F
I G N R I I A V
X S T E A
O O O A D R L C

PUZZLE 36

The above are anagrams of the names of American states. Can you work them out?

See answer 113

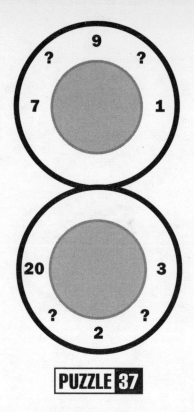

PUZZLE 37

Can you work out whether + or − should replace the question marks in this diagram so that both sections arrive at the same value?

See answer 136

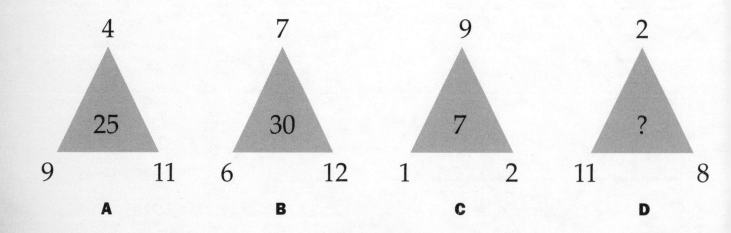

PUZZLE 38

The above triangles follow a pattern. Can you work it out and find the missing number?

See answer 97

Jim sat in the bedroom watching the never-ending rain morosely.

It had fallen on his home town for three weeks without cease and there were now floods everywhere.

In most places the water was several feet deep and rising rapidly.

Everyone had been forced to live upstairs.

Just then his wife walked in but, try as he might, Jim couldn't get her to take the situation seriously.

Why not?

See answer **42**

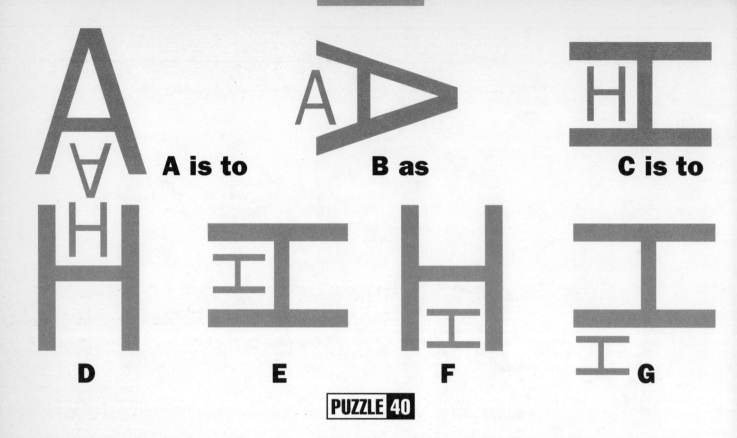

A is to   B as   C is to

D   E   F   G

PUZZLE 40

See answer 110

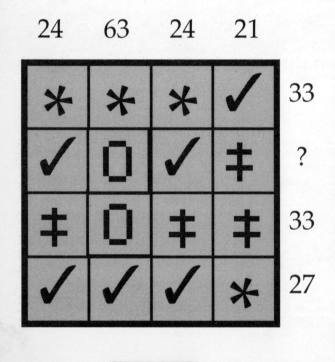

24   63   24   21

33
?
33
27

PUZZLE 41

Each symbol in this square represents a value. Can you work out how much the question mark is worth?

See answer 94

NUCXW SXQW
OANMMRN VNALDAH
URBJ BCJWBORNUM
BRWNJM X'LXWWXA
VNJCUXJO
VJMXWWJ
VRLQJNU SJLTBXW
AXM BCNFJAC

PUZZLE 42

The above is a simple substitution code which conceals the names of eight pop singers. See if you can work out who they are.

See answer 109

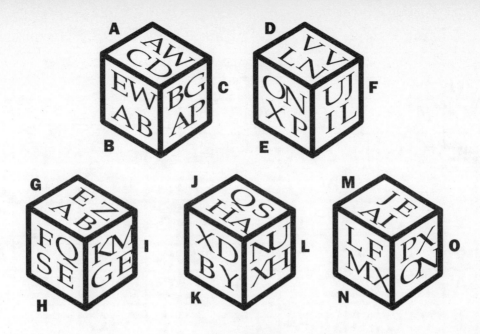

PUZZLE 43

Two sides of these cubes contain the same letters. Can you spot them?

See answer 82

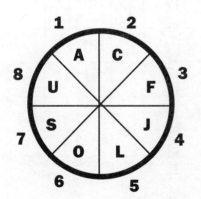 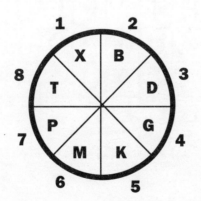 

PUZZLE 44

Can you find the letter which fits in the missing segment?

See answer 16

C	W	C	O	A	L	M	K	W	O	E	A	C	K	L	G	O	Z	A	N
L	H	E	M	I	N	G	W	A	Y	N	E	I	Y	L	M	O	X	A	E
L	E	E	C	M	O	X	K	W	A	X	F	E	X	A	N	B	K	O	S
C	F	A	K	K	E	N	Z	A	E	X	L	A	E	B	L	P	E	F	B
A	I	E	L	H	M	Z	N	O	E	X	I	A	I	F	H	R	K	L	I
M	O	Q	V	T	O	A	T	E	U	I	W	E	H	T	E	O	G	M	O
A	T	K	V	L	A	V	C	H	A	E	M	N	O	L	E	U	A	B	C
F	S	I	A	T	A	M	Q	L	S	D	I	C	K	E	N	S	S	T	A
A	L	S	T	V	E	M	W	M	N	O	E	I	A	C	H	T	A	C	T
F	O	O	X	W	A	B	E	A	L	L	E	I	T	A	W	W	A	C	G
G	T	O	X	A	E	A	K	F	A	K	I	L	A	A	S	T	A	W	N
O	N	F	B	C	H	J	K	W	L	L	T	J	I	I	E	X	G	H	I
E	N	O	L	F	M	G	O	Z	X	A	Y	N	A	E	B	E	C	W	L
R	V	O	L	F	I	G	A	E	Z	I	U	I	E	J	C	C	K	T	P
E	W	U	V	E	C	U	O	P	T	E	G	B	P	N	H	T	S	E	I
C	S	E	W	X	H	L	H	J	A	L	E	C	E	K	L	T	U	Z	K
U	A	T	A	E	E	C	K	U	W	P	Q	R	A	R	A	E	P	A	Z
A	U	S	T	E	N	X	A	T	A	Q	W	A	L	E	T	A	W	V	E
H	A	P	E	X	E	A	B	C	B	A	C	A	E	W	W	E	X	L	E
C	C	W	A	O	R	W	E	L	L	K	M	N	O	P	P	E	L	T	U

Austen	Hemingway	Michener
Chaucer	Huxley	Orwell
Chekhov	Ibsen	Proust
Dickens	Kafka	Tolstoi
Flaubert	Kipling	Twain
Goethe	Lawrence	Zola

PUZZLE 45

In this grid are hidden the names of 18 famous authors. Can you detect them? You can go forward or in reverse, in horizontal, vertical and diagonal lines.

See answer 38

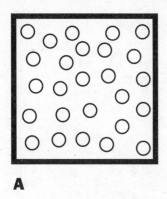 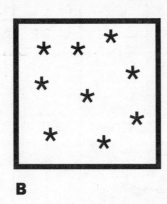  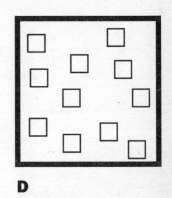

A **B** **C** **D**

PUZZLE 46

There is a logic to the patterns in these squares but one does not fit. Can you find the odd one out?

See answer 3

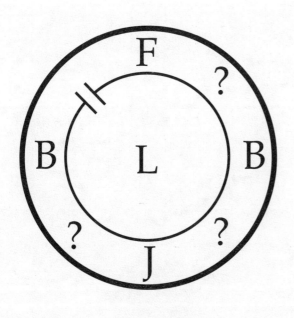

PUZZLE 47

Can you work out which mathematical signs should replace the question marks in this diagram? You have a choice between – or +.

See answer 10

PUZZLE 48

Which letter replaces the question mark in this star?

See answer 30

PUZZLE 49

These tiles, when placed in right order, will form
a square in which each horizontal line is
identical with one vertical line.
Can you successfully form the square?

See answer 88

PUZZLE 50

Can you work out what the time on the
blank clock face should be?

See answer 20

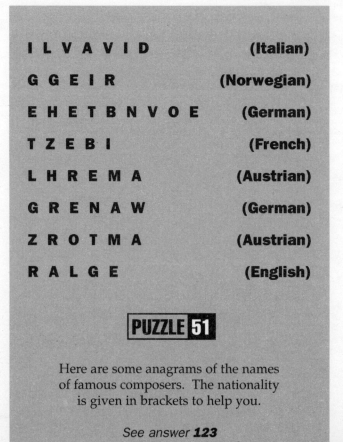

I L V A V I D   (Italian)

G G E I R   (Norwegian)

E H E T B N V O E   (German)

T Z E B I   (French)

L H R E M A   (Austrian)

G R E N A W   (German)

Z R O T M A   (Austrian)

R A L G E   (English)

PUZZLE 51

Here are some anagrams of the names
of famous composers. The nationality
is given in brackets to help you.

See answer 123

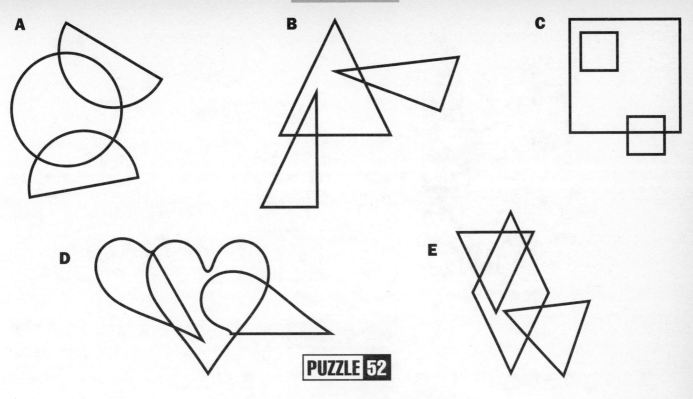

A B C

D E

PUZZLE 52

Can you work out which of these diagram is
different from the others?

See answer 138

1 3 2 6 4 12 8 24 ?

PUZZLE 53

What comes next in this sequence?

See answer 63

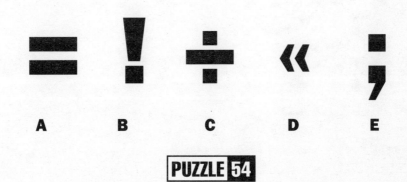

A B C D E

PUZZLE 54

Can you work out which of these symbols
is the odd one out?

See answer 140

41 34 12 14 52 52 42
53 24 44 13 53 14 43 11 51
22 14 64 22 34 43
31 24 42 43 14 53 11 42
12 42 43 52 51 14 13 31 24
53 14 41 21 14 24 31
63 14 43 22 42 22 21
44 14 51 34 52 52 24

PUZZLE 55

This is a simple grid code. The encoded words are all
names of famous painters.

See answer 115

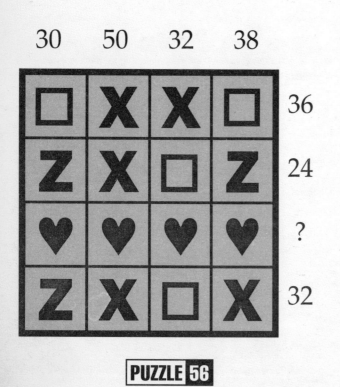

PUZZLE 56

Each symbol in the above square represents a number.
Can you find out how much the question
mark is worth?

See answer 98

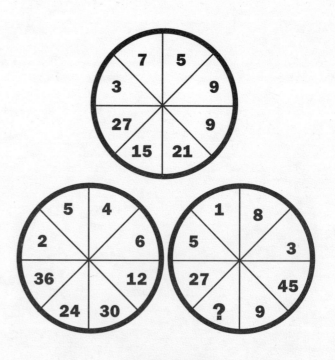

PUZZLE 57

Can you find the missing number that fits into
the sector of the last wheel?

See answer 55

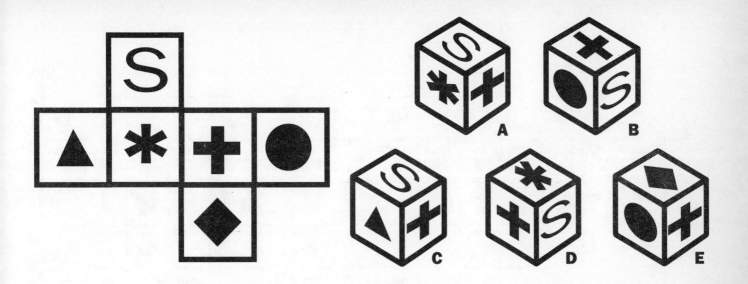

PUZZLE 58

Which of these cubes cannot be made
from this layout?

See answer 36

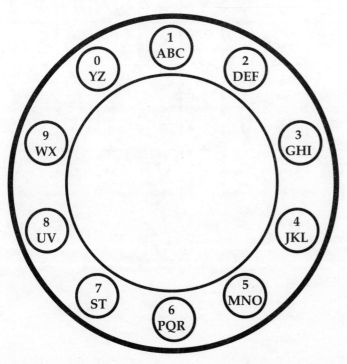

PUZZLE 59

The diagram represent an old-fashioned telephone
dial with letters as well as numbers. Below is a list of
numbers representing 10 American towns or cities.
Can you decode them?

See answer 48

A.	214417	F.	65674152
B.	7217742	G.	2276537
C.	1331135	H.	1741571
D.	534918422	I.	1351355173
E.	53552165437	J.	352315165437

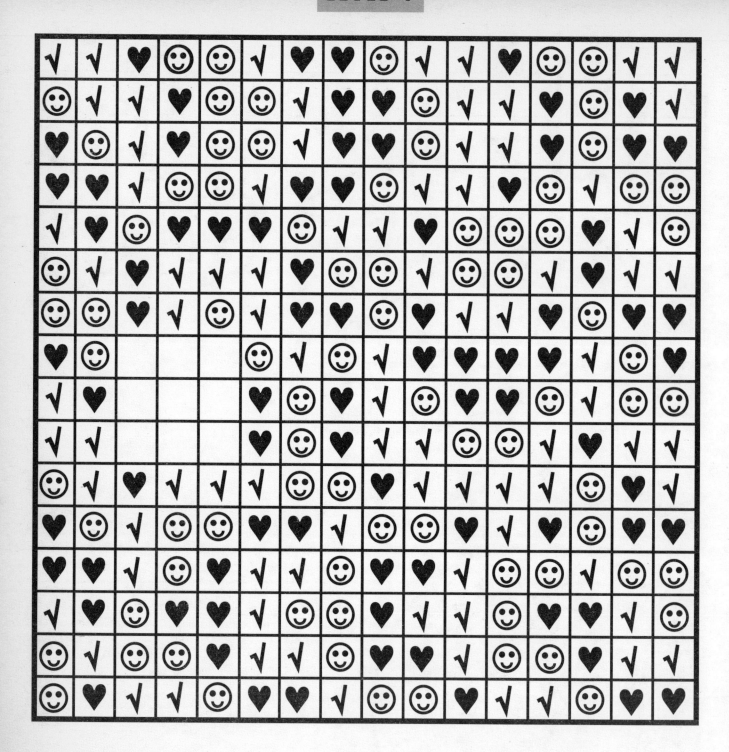

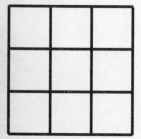

PUZZLE 60

The symbols in the above grid follow a pattern. Can you work it out and find the missing section?

See answer **60**

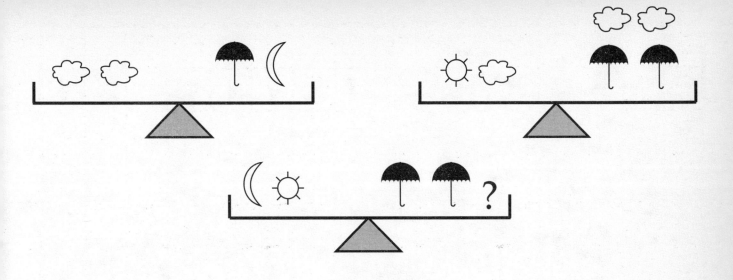

PUZZLE 61

The first two sets of scales are in balance.
Which symbol is needed to balance the third set?

See answer 5

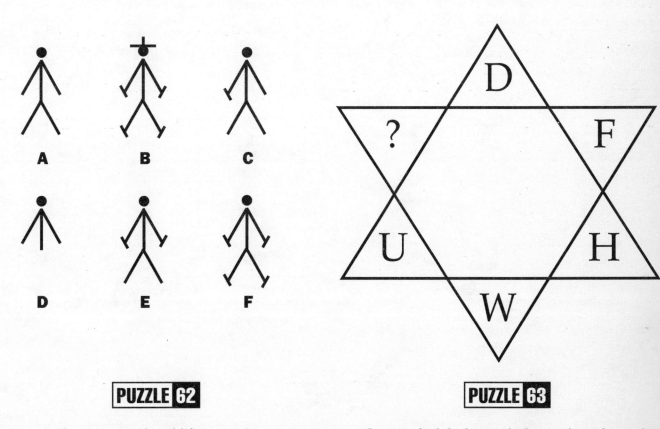

PUZZLE 62

Can you spot the odd figure out?

See answer 137

PUZZLE 63

Can you find the letter which completes the star?

See answer 47

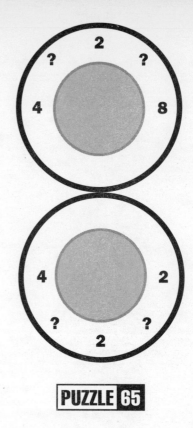

ΜΙΥΥΜΕ ΙΥΑΜΥ
ΗΣΕΕΞΨΙΓΘ ΧΙΜΜΑΗΕ
ΝΑΞΘΑΥΥΑΞ
ΥΙΝΕΤ ΤΡΦΑΣΕ
ΗΣΑΝΕΣΓΥ ΠΑΣΛ
ΤΟΘΟ
ΓΕΞΥΣΑΜ ΠΑΣΛ
ΓΘΙΞΑΥΟΨΕ

PUZZLE 64

Above are the coded names of some places in New York. Can you work out their names? Vowels A, E, I and O are correct.

See answer 75

PUZZLE 65

Can you work out what mathematical signs should replace the question marks so that both sections of the diagram arrive at the same value. You have a choice between ÷ or x.

See answer 89

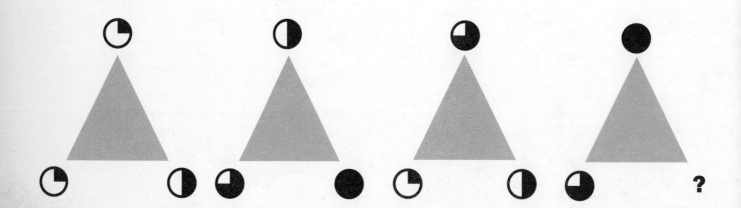

PUZZLE 66

Can you find the missing symbol in the last triangle?

See answer 76

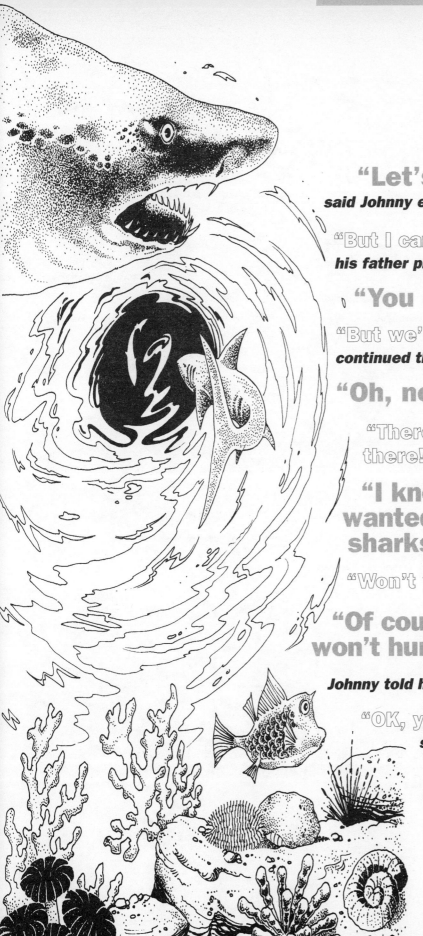

PUZZLE 67

"Let's go under the sea!"
said Johnny excitedly to his dad.

"But I can't swim,"
his father protested.

"You don't have to."

"But we'll get wet,"
continued the reluctant parent.

"Oh, no we won't."

"There are sharks down there!"

"I know – I've always wanted to see real sharks!"

"Won't you be scared?"

"Of course not, they won't hurt us."

Johnny told his dad where he meant to go.

"OK, you win,"
said the relieved parent.

"Let's go!"
said Johnny.

Johnny and his dad are not going diving, or taking a trip in a glass-bottomed boat. So how are they going under the sea without coming to any harm?

See answer 45

XII + XVII = XLV

PUZZLE 68

MATCH POINTS
Can you correct this sum by moving four matches?

See answer 26

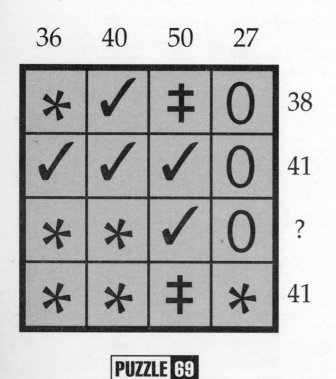

PUZZLE 69

Each symbol in this square represents a value.
Can you find out which number should replace the
question mark?

See answer 23

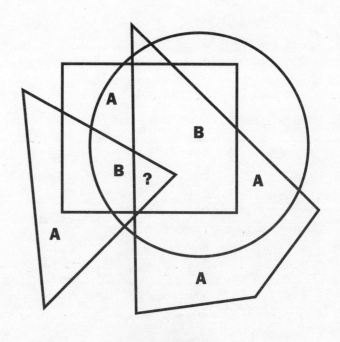

PUZZLE 70

A certain logic has been used in making this diagram.
Can you work out what the secret is and replace the
question mark with a letter?

See answer 131

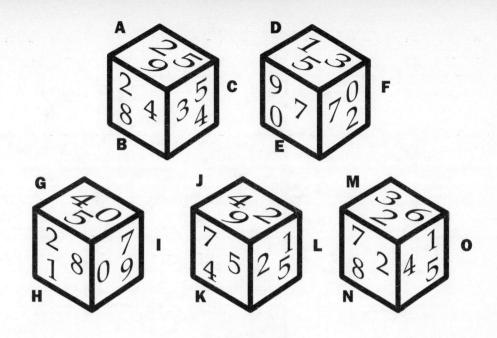

PUZZLE 71

Two sides on these cubes contain the same numbers.
Can you spot them?

See answer 107

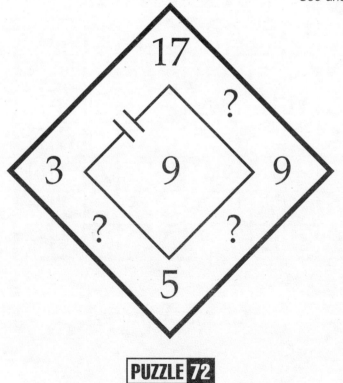

PUZZLE 72

The mathematical signs in this diamond have been
left out. Reading clockwise from the top can you work
out what the question marks stand for?

See answer 108

PUZZLE 73

OPLNNOEA   (France)
RCLUCHIHL   (GB)
MATNRU   (USA)
EDLAGELU   (France)
NNEEYDK   (USA)
OHHICHNIM   (Vietnam)
INHDAG   (India)
LEDAANM   (South Africa)

Here are anagrams of famous statesmen. Their
nationalities are given to help you.

See answer 37

P	B	A	W	N	W	O	C	H	K	T	V	E	N	T	A	C	Y	X	O
A	A	D	E	F	W	O	Y	J	U	L	I	A	R	O	B	E	R	T	S
C	D	U	S	T	I	N	H	O	F	F	M	A	N	B	R	M	O	N	L
K	A	O	L	W	O	L	N	N	Y	G	O	R	E	S	O	T	U	V	D
K	M	G	E	N	E	W	I	L	D	E	R	W	O	L	O	Z	B	R	R
C	A	S	K	L	E	M	U	O	T	L	B	W	J	L	K	K	E	G	O
P	C	M	W	V	U	W	E	A	I	J	L	G	A	H	E	T	E	B	F
E	L	K	E	F	O	Z	M	A	A	T	H	E	N	A	S	E	R	O	D
E	S	O	A	L	L	A	M	A	A	O	I	E	E	O	H	I	L	L	E
R	T	A	S	E	G	F	A	A	N	T	O	E	F	L	I	S	T	R	R
T	O	M	C	R	U	I	S	E	S	R	S	E	O	T	E	E	E	P	T
S	A	O	E	E	B	W	B	I	M	Q	I	A	N	E	L	G	N	O	R
L	A	A	O	H	E	H	R	S	T	D	A	B	D	C	D	O	A	T	E
Y	A	F	G	S	V	H	T	E	O	I	B	K	A	R	S	C	E	J	B
R	B	P	O	A	C	F	A	J	Z	N	A	Y	A	A	Y	I	X	Q	O
E	N	O	Z	E	A	L	M	A	O	C	Y	H	F	O	G	H	E	L	R
M	A	E	I	N	A	Z	E	N	I	A	C	L	E	A	H	C	I	M	B
C	P	L	M	A	N	N	V	W	X	I	E	R	S	F	L	A	Z	O	N
N	U	W	M	J	F	G	Q	S	R	A	E	L	L	A	E	S	S	O	E
J	O	N	Y	F	G	I	N	O	S	P	M	O	H	T	A	M	M	E	F

Jane Asher

Julia Roberts

Mel Gibson

Julie Christie

Meryl Streep

Paul Newman

Jane Fonda

Gene Wilder

Richard Gere

Michael Caine

Brooke Shields

Dustin Hoffman

Tom Cruise

Emma Thompson

Robert Redford

Jodie Foster

PUZZLE 74

Hidden in this grid are the names of 16 well-known actors. Can you spot them? You can move in horizontal, vertical and diagonal lines in a forward or backward direction.

See answer 61

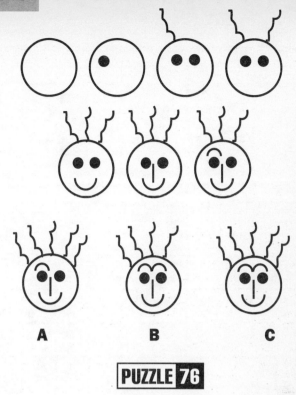

JWQA LM JWCTWOVM
UWVBXIZVIAAM
UILMTMQVM
XMZM TIKPIQAM
KPIUXA MTGAMMA
OIZM LM TGWV
IZK LM BZQWUXPM
UWVBU IZBZM

PUZZLE 75

Here are the coded names of some places in Paris.
Can you discover their identity?

See answer 66

A   B   C

PUZZLE 76

Which of the following faces, A, B or C, would carry
on the sequence above?

See answer 90

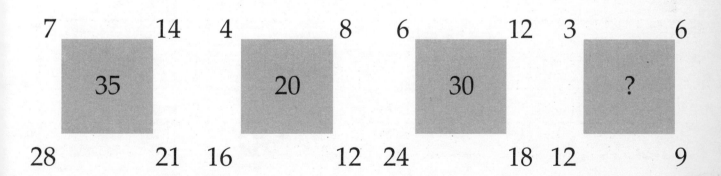

7   14   4   8   6   12   3   6

35   20   30   ?

28   21   16   12   24   18   12   9

PUZZLE 77

Can you work out which number should go into
the last square?

See answer 52

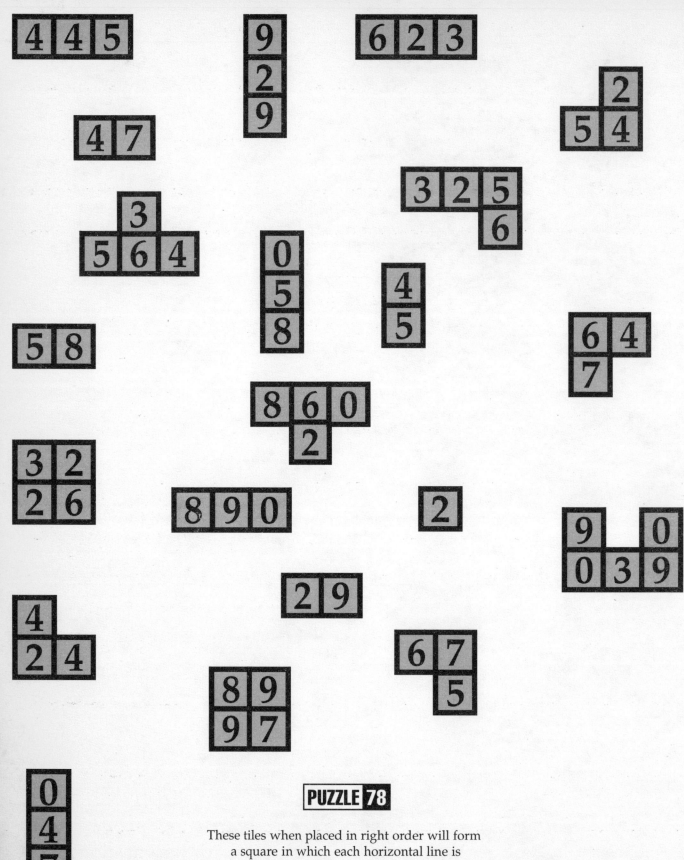

PUZZLE 78

These tiles when placed in right order will form
a square in which each horizontal line is
identical with one vertical line.
Can you successfully form the square?

See answer 77

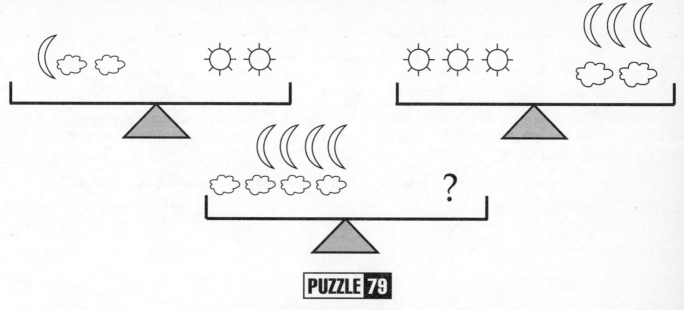

PUZZLE 79

Can you work out which symbols you need
to balance the scale?

See answer 31

PUZZLE 80

Can you work out what the blank clockface
should look like?

See answer 64

AJILU TREBORS
RUBT NOYLEDRS
CAKJ OHLCSIONN
VDAID EVNIN
IRLANYM RNOOME
MERYJE NSORI
URYEDA BPEHRNU
NNOAIW DYRER

PUZZLE 81

The above are anagrams of the names of film
stars. Both the first and second names are given.

See answer 132

A is to **B** as **C** is to

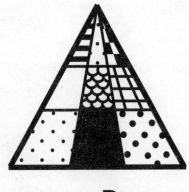 

D **E**

 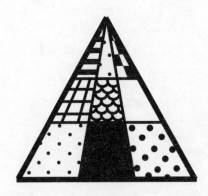

F **G**

PUZZLE 82

See answer 121

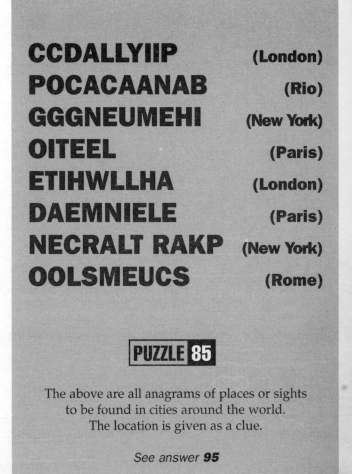

PUZZLE 83

Can you find the two sides on these cubes which
contain exactly the same symbols?

See answer 134

36   23   24   ?

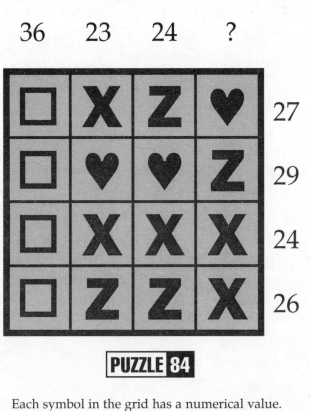

27

29

24

26

PUZZLE 84

Each symbol in the grid has a numerical value.
Work out what those values are and replace the
question mark with a number.

See answer 7

CCDALLYIIP	(London)
POCACAANAB	(Rio)
GGGNEUMEHI	(New York)
OITEEL	(Paris)
ETIHWLLHA	(London)
DAEMNIELE	(Paris)
NECRALT RAKP	(New York)
OOLSMEUCS	(Rome)

PUZZLE 85

The above are all anagrams of places or sights
to be found in cities around the world.
The location is given as a clue.

See answer 95

K	L	N	B	C	E	W	O	P	Q	B	A	I	K	M	O	L	C
G	A	E	C	C	W	V	R	A	E	I	X	C	M	O	L	A	D
B	E	F	H	A	E	L	E	H	A	R	U	O	H	N	K	M	X
O	A	B	A	C	H	A	N	A	E	X	T	A	T	O	T	E	W
R	L	O	N	E	F	A	G	E	T	W	Y	A	E	X	P	M	M
O	N	A	D	E	A	G	A	H	A	D	H	E	L	L	E	I	E
D	A	C	E	F	G	E	W	A	N	E	A	E	I	M	C	O	N
I	U	F	L	I	S	Z	T	B	E	N	T	V	O	W	L	C	D
N	A	E	K	M	O	Z	G	A	V	E	A	Z	C	K	L	P	E
Q	S	K	A	E	K	E	B	E	O	H	A	R	T	U	E	K	L
L	W	A	A	E	I	P	Q	R	H	R	A	E	T	X	C	K	S
A	C	E	I	R	V	O	S	P	T	Q	V	R	W	B	R	C	S
S	D	A	G	E	O	K	W	O	E	L	X	I	M	N	U	T	O
M	O	V	X	Z	K	V	M	N	E	K	E	C	V	A	P	J	H
H	L	W	X	Q	W	A	D	E	B	U	S	S	Y	A	T	O	N
A	O	W	P	X	B	E	I	E	P	Q	O	Z	A	C	L	T	W
R	A	C	A	S	C	H	U	B	E	R	T	T	O	R	H	D	A
B	B	C	F	K	L	M	N	T	A	C	T	O	A	R	Z	W	I

PUZZLE 86

Bach	**Dvorak**	**Mendelssohn**
Beethoven	**Grieg**	**Mozart**
Borodin	**Handel**	**Purcell**
Brahms	**Haydn**	**Schubert**
Chopin	**Lehar**	**Vivaldi**
Debussy	**Liszt**	**Wagner**

Hidden in this grid are 18 names of well-known composers. Can you find them? You can move horizontally, vertically or diagonally and in a forward or backward direction.

See answer 68

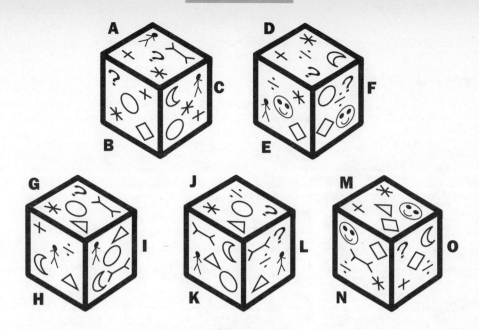

PUZZLE 87

There are two sides on those cubes that contain exactly
the same symbols. Can you spot them?

See answer 99

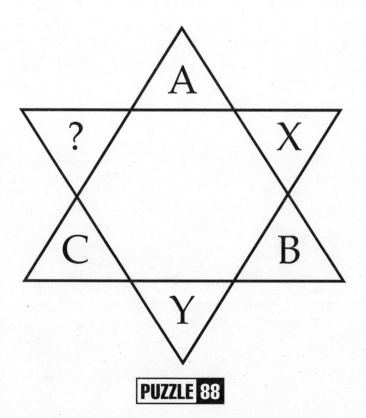

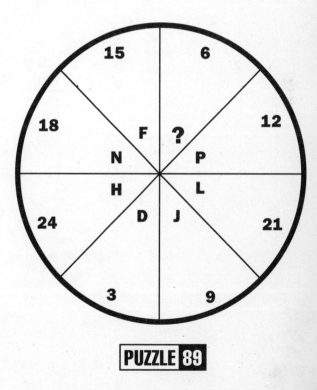

PUZZLE 89

The letters and numbers in this wheel are related in
some way. Can you find which letter should replace
the question mark?

See answer 18

PUZZLE 88

Can you find the letter to complete the star?

See answer 86

VMASIO (American)
ZLBACA (French)
YHAEWMGIN (American)
CYOEJ (Irish)
MHUAMAG (English)
RELIML (American)
STRUPO (French)
NWITA (American)

PUZZLE 90

The above are anagrams of the names of famous novelists. The nationality is given in brackets to help you.

See answer 141

? 7 4 8 9 0
3 5 0 2 6 7
1 2 4 6 2 3

PUZZLE 91

Can you find the missing number which would complete the diagram?

See answer 34

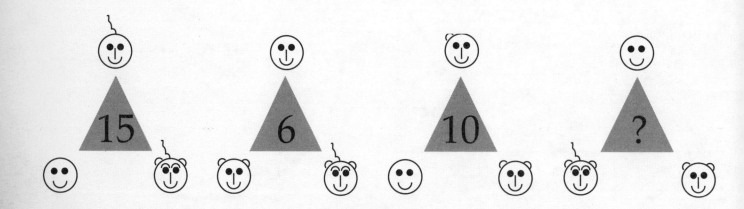

PUZZLE 92

Can you work out which number the question mark in the triangle stands for?

See answer 24

Dr Arnold Gluck, a psychiatrist in New York, came across the world's most enthusiastic bookworm during the course of his work.

He had been one since infancy. All he ever did was devour books.

Yet he never held down a proper job and he didn't go to the public library.

He hadn't inherited money, in fact he was penniless.

So how could he get through all those books?

See answer 44

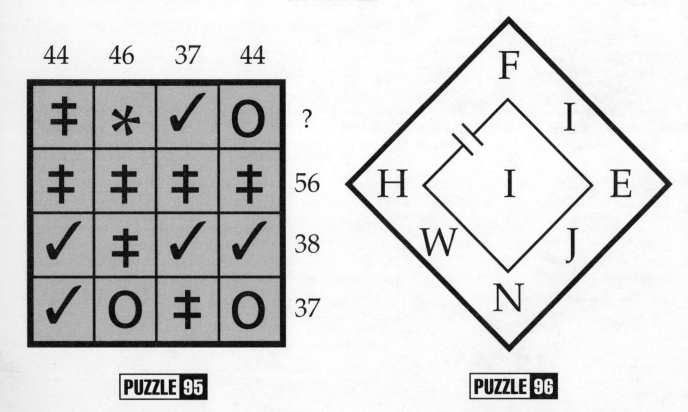

A   is to   B   as   C   is to

D   E   F   G

PUZZLE 94

See answer 116

PUZZLE 95

Each symbol in this square represents a number. Can you work out which number should replace the question mark?

See answer 78

PUZZLE 96

In this diagram the mathematical signs (+ and − only) between each letter (which has a value equal to its position in the alphabet) have gone missing. Can you restore them in a way that you arrive at the letter in the middle of the diamond?

See answer 53

PUZZLE 97

Can you find the two sides on these cubes that contain
exactly the same symbols?

See answer 125

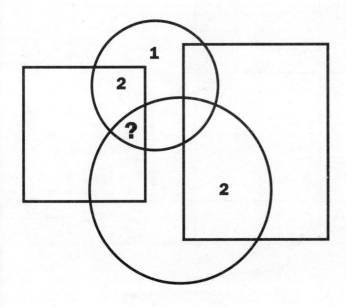

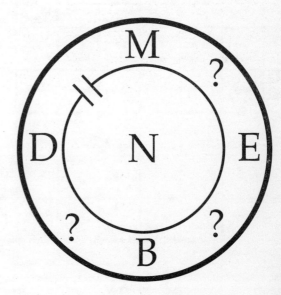

PUZZLE 98

PUZZLE 99

This diagram was constructed according to a certain
logic. Can you work out which number should
replace the question mark?

Can you work out whether + or − should replace the
question mark to arrive at the letter in the middle of
the circle?

See answer 124

See answer 143

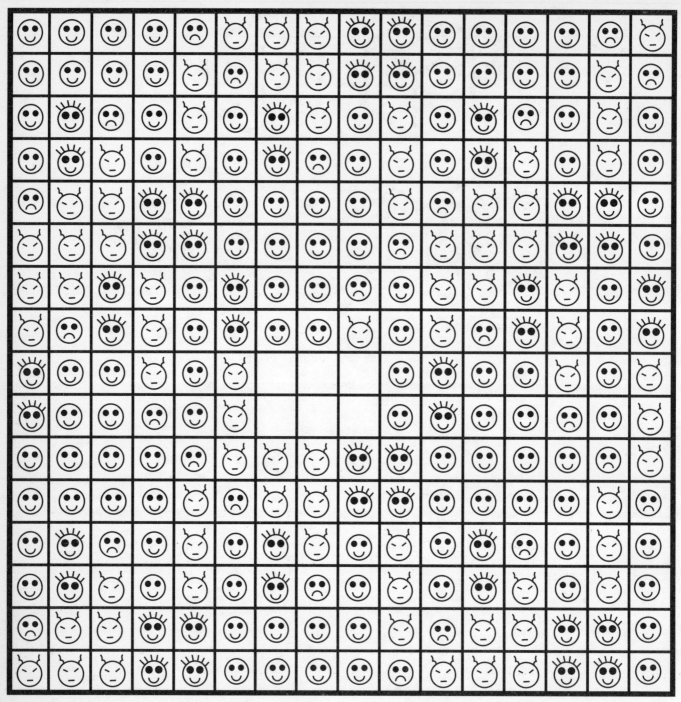

 **A**

 **B**

PUZZLE 100

The symbols in the above grid follow a pattern. Can you work it out and find the missing section?

See answer 84

 **C**

D

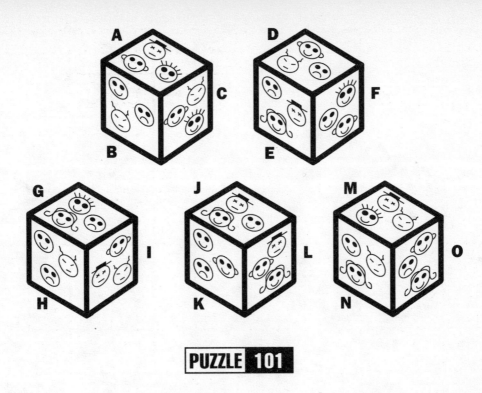

PUZZLE 101

Can you work out which two sides on these cubes
contain the same symbols?

See answer 13

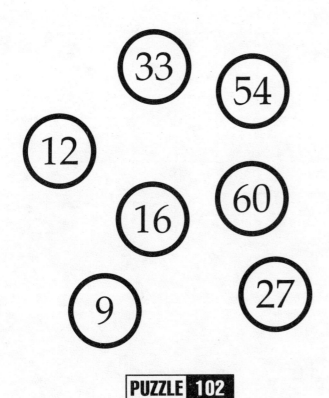

PUZZLE 102

Can you work out which is the odd ball out?

See answer 71

ΨΘΙΥΕΘΑΜΜ
ΥΣΑΖΑΜΗΑΣ ΤΡΦΑΣΕ
ΛΕΞΤΙΞΗΥΟΞ ΗΑΣΔΕΞΤ
ΝΑΣΒΜΕ ΑΣΓΘ
ΒΦΓΛΙΞΗΘΑΝ ΠΑΜΑΓΕ
ΠΙΓΓΑΔΙΜΜΥ ΓΙΣΓΦΤ
ΗΣΟΤΧΕΞΟΣ ΤΡΦΑΣΕ
ΥΘΑΝΕΤ ΕΝΒΑΞΛΝΕΞΥ
ΨΑΥΕΣΜΟΟ ΤΥΑΥΙΟΞ
ΛΙΞΗΤ ΓΣΟΤΤ

PUZZLE 103

The above are the coded names of places in London.
Can you decode them? Only the vowels
A, E, I, and O and consonant B are correct.

See answer 54

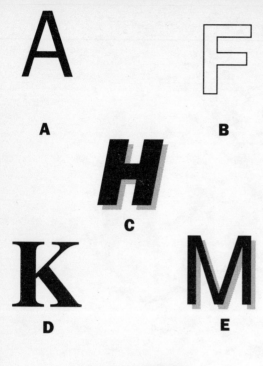

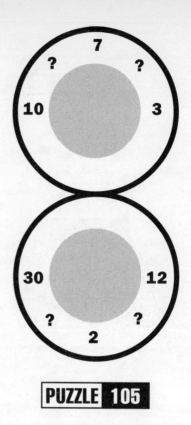

PUZZLE 104

Can you work out which of these letters is the odd one out?

See answer 133

PUZZLE 105

Can you replace the question marks with + or – so that both sections in this diagram add up to the same value.

See answer 126

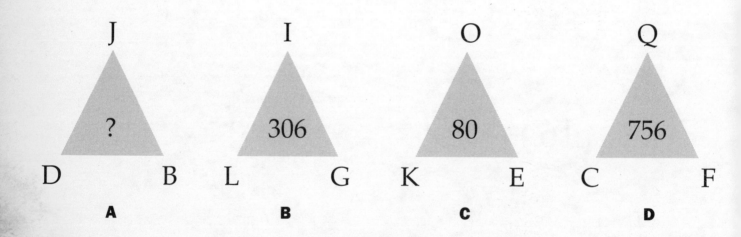

PUZZLE 106

Can you work out which number fits into the first triangle?

See answer 56

A man came home to find himself locked out of his house and his back yard full of water.

An upstairs window was open, but he had

no ladder to help him reach it.

However, if he could just

reach the top of his

front porch he'd be able to

reach the window.

Then he had an idea.

What was it?

It did not involve ladders, steps or

climbing up the walls of the house.

See answer **40**

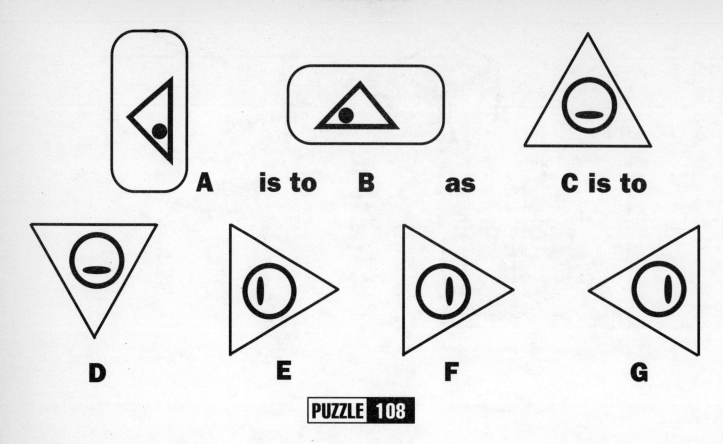

A   is to   B   as   C is to

D   E   F   G

PUZZLE 108

See answer 8

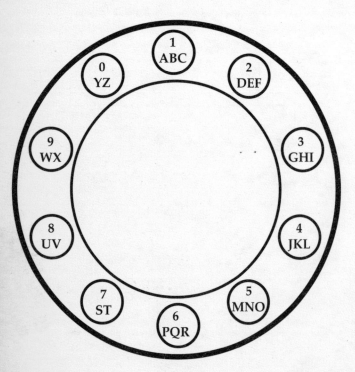

PUZZLE 109

The diagram represents an old-fashioned telephone dial with letters as well as numbers. Below is a list of numbers representing 10 large cities from around the world. Can you use the diagram to decode them?

See answer 92

A.	5151327726	**F.**	1153454
B.	3417359	**G.**	11418771
C.	75845872	**H.**	524158652
D.	75542574	**I.**	116124551
E.	815158826	**J.**	7116152575

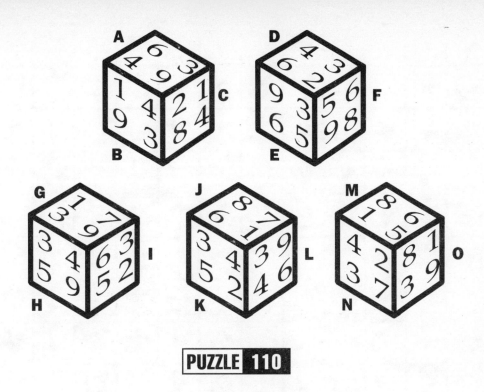

Two sides of these cubes contain exactly the same
numbers. Can you spot them?

See answer 57

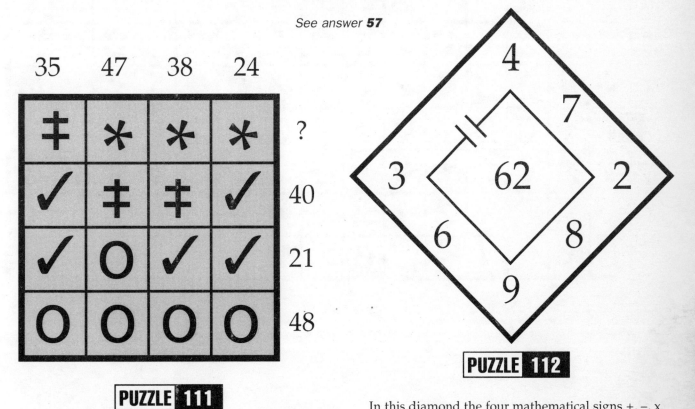

Can you work out what number each symbol
represents and find the value of the question mark?

See answer 59

In this diamond the four mathematical signs +, −, x
and ÷ have been left out. Can you work out which
sign fits between each pair of numbers to arrive at the
number in the middle of the diagram?

See answer 17

♥	√	√	Ø	Ø	‡	♥	√	√	Ø	Ø	‡	♥	√	√	Ø
♥	♥	Ø	√	‡	‡	♥	♥	Ø	√	‡	‡	♥	♥	Ø	√
√	‡	‡	♥	♥	Ø	√	‡	‡	♥	♥	Ø	√	‡	‡	♥
Ø	Ø	‡	♥	√	√	Ø	Ø	‡	♥	√	√	Ø	Ø	‡	♥
Ø	Ø	♥	‡	√	√	Ø	Ø	♥	‡	√	√	Ø	Ø	♥	‡
‡	√	♥	‡	Ø				♥	‡	Ø	♥	‡	√	♥	‡
♥	♥	√	Ø	‡			√	Ø	‡	‡	♥	♥	√	Ø	
√	♥	Ø	√	‡			Ø	√	‡	Ø	√	♥	Ø	√	
√	‡	Ø	√	♥	Ø	√	‡	Ø	√	♥	Ø	√	‡	Ø	√
Ø	‡	‡	♥	♥	√	Ø	‡	‡	♥	♥	√	Ø	‡	‡	♥
‡	Ø	♥	‡	√	♥	‡	Ø	♥	‡	√	♥	‡	Ø	♥	‡
‡	√	√	Ø	Ø	♥	‡	√	√	Ø	Ø	♥	‡	√	√	Ø
♥	√	√	Ø	Ø	‡	♥	√	√	Ø	Ø	‡	♥	√	√	Ø
♥	♥	Ø	√	‡	‡	♥	♥	Ø	√	‡	‡	♥	♥	Ø	√
√	‡	‡	♥	♥	Ø	√	‡	‡	♥	♥	Ø	√	‡	‡	♥
Ø	Ø	‡	♥	√	√	Ø	Ø	‡	♥	√	√	Ø	Ø	‡	♥

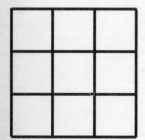

PUZZLE 113

The symbols in this grid follow a pattern. Can you
work it out and complete the missing section?

See answer 74

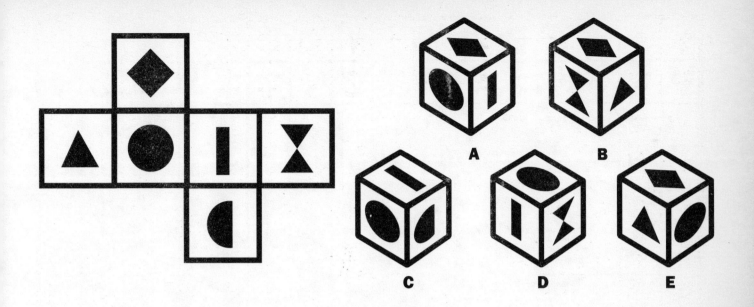

PUZZLE 114

Which of these cubes cannot be made from this layout?

See answer 65

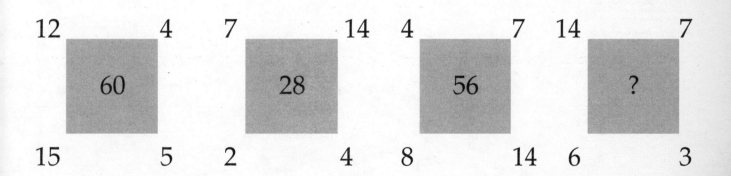

PUZZLE 115

Can you work out the number needed to complete the square?

See answer 80

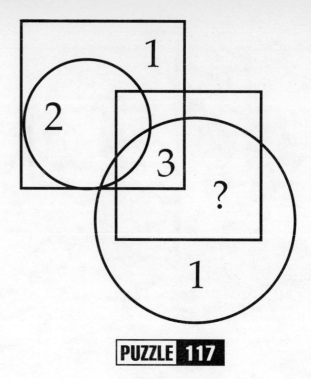

PUZZLE 116

Can you find the mathematical signs which should
replace the question marks in this diagram?

See answer **129**

PUZZLE 117

Can you crack the logic of this diagram and replace
the question mark with a number?

See answer **112**

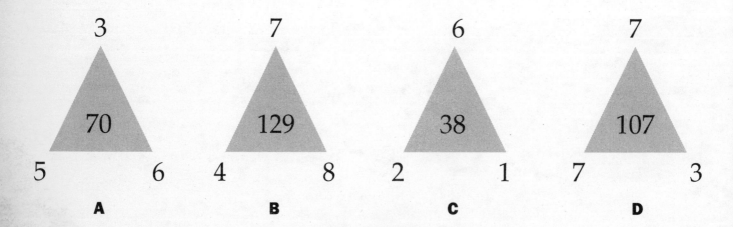

PUZZLE 118

The four triangles are linked by a simple mathematical
formula. Can you discover what it is and then find
the odd one out?

See answer **2**

PUZZLE 119

Old Silas Greenfield died and left each of his grandchildren the same bequest.

Sam spent all his having a good time, Dave wasted his and Suzy used hers wisely.

The old man had been determined to treat the grandchildren equally, and in a way he did, **but each got a different sum of money.**

Why?

See answer 43

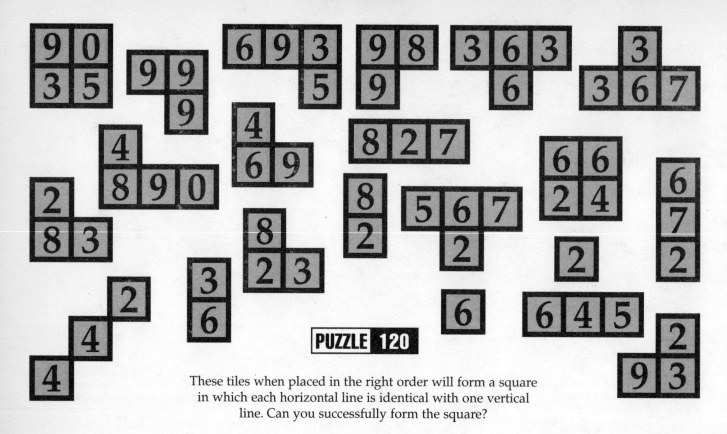

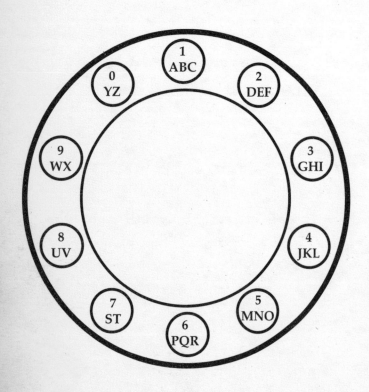

PUZZLE 120

These tiles when placed in the right order will form a square in which each horizontal line is identical with one vertical line. Can you successfully form the square?

See answer 85

PUZZLE 121

The diagram represents an old-fashioned telephone dial with letters as well as numbers. Below is a list of numbers representing 10 international capital cities. Can you use the diagram to decode them?

See answer 79

A.	1562531325	F.	157726215
B.	661382	G.	775143545
C.	455255	H.	1545515
D.	126435	I.	512632
E.	75405	J.	154161

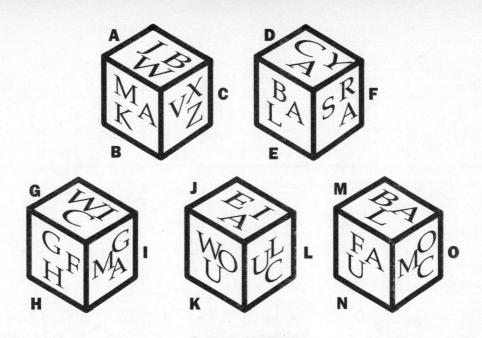

PUZZLE 122

Can you work out which sides on these cubes contain
the same letters?

See answer 142

22 8 10 20 14 5 2 7
9 20 24 5 5 20
23 2 6 12 14 6
12 14 12 1 2
21 11 20 13 16 14 11 12 13
1 20 6 21 14 11 26 24 11
12 9 20 26 1 24 13 13 2
15 2 7 23 20 5 8 8

PUZZLE 123

This is a simple substitution code that uses
numbers instead of letters. The coded words are all
well-known foods from around the world.

See answer 135

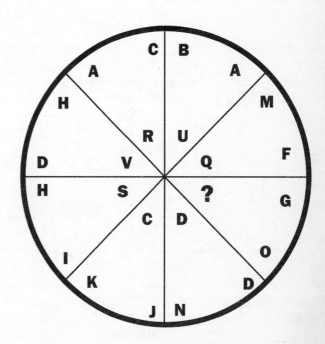

PUZZLE 124

Can you find out which letter completes the wheel?

See answer 29

```
M O X A L T E F E I C H A L P X N O N S
F A L E F T I E X W K C R A M S I B P X
A L L L I H C R U H C E T P W O L I J L
M O N E D A L O X E G H N X E F A L A E
A X O N A E C E A L E I S P E E T F A E
G I A A O N E A B C A F I A A W S U P V
N G T E A A I Y D E N N E K O U S L E E
U S A R G H A N F A O S E L T A I X O H
T P F E Q R A A E C S E F A L N T A U C
E F A H S R A E H E A E N A C H I A E A
S A E C E A F E A E O N S O A T N A F B
T L O T A O T E A D F A L P E R I T O R
O L T A A S A A F E G N A E R L L O M O
A I N H O F S A F G P Q R N A E O M E G
M E A T B C E A D A D A U I F O S P X M
L M O X M N O P Q U R S T S A U S X A O
W V A E X F O H J L A A T T U B U C W N
O Z X A E F A O Z L A E H L U F M R A Z
A E N O I R U G N E B F A E E A K L M N
O Z A D A C A H P T S R S Y T R A E L M
```

Arafat **Gandhi**

Mussolini **Ben Gurion**

Gorbachev **Napoleon**

Bismarck **Kennedy**

Pinochet **Churchill**

Lincoln **Stalin**

De Gaulle **Mao Tse Tung**

Thatcher **Franco**

Mitterand **Yeltsin**

PUZZLE 125

The above grid contains the names of 18 famous statesmen. Can you discover them?

See answer 93

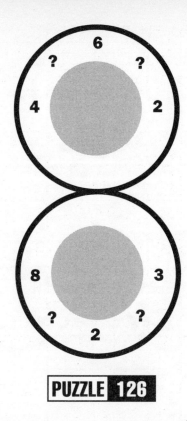

PUZZLE 126

Can you replace the question marks in this diagram with either X or ÷ so that both sections arrive at the same value?

See answer 117

PUZZLE 127

Can you work out which of these balls is the odd one out?

See answer 111

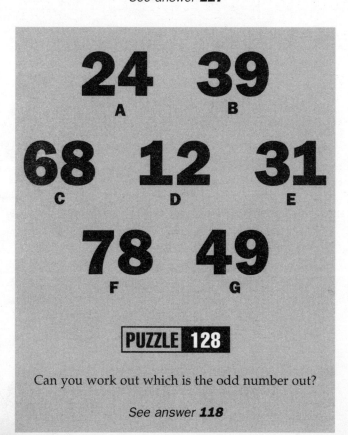

PUZZLE 128

Can you work out which is the odd number out?

See answer 118

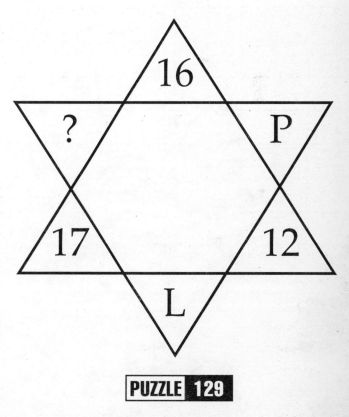

PUZZLE 129

Can you find the missing letter in this star?

See answer 70

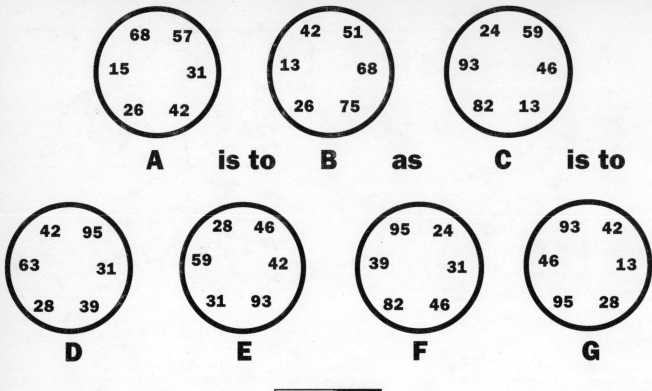

A   is to   B   as   C   is to

D   E   F   G

PUZZLE 130

See answer 103

A D G J ?
H L P T ?
U Z E J ?

PUZZLE 131

Each of the lines in this diagram follows a pattern.
Can you find the missing letters?

See answer 72

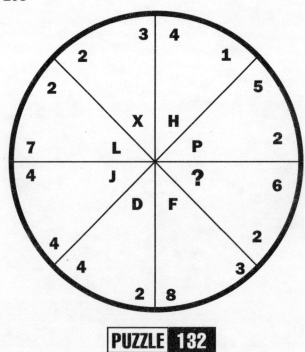

PUZZLE 132

Can you unravel the reasoning behind
this diagram and find the correct letter to replace
the question mark?

See answer 4

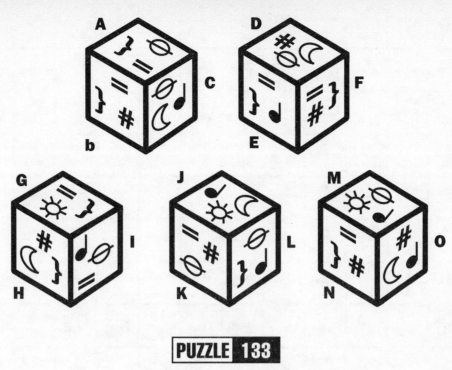

PUZZLE 133

Can you work out which three sides of these cubes
contain the same symbols?

See answer 102

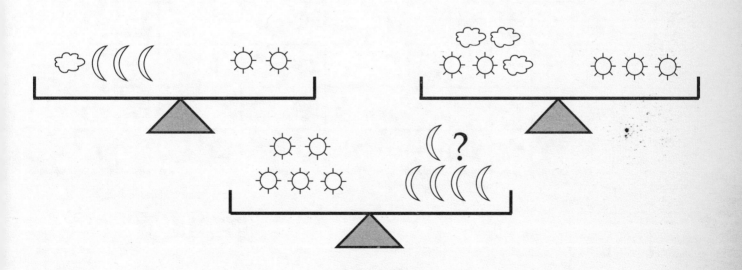

PUZZLE 134

Each of the symbols represents a value. Which symbols
would you need to add to balance the last scale?

See answer 14

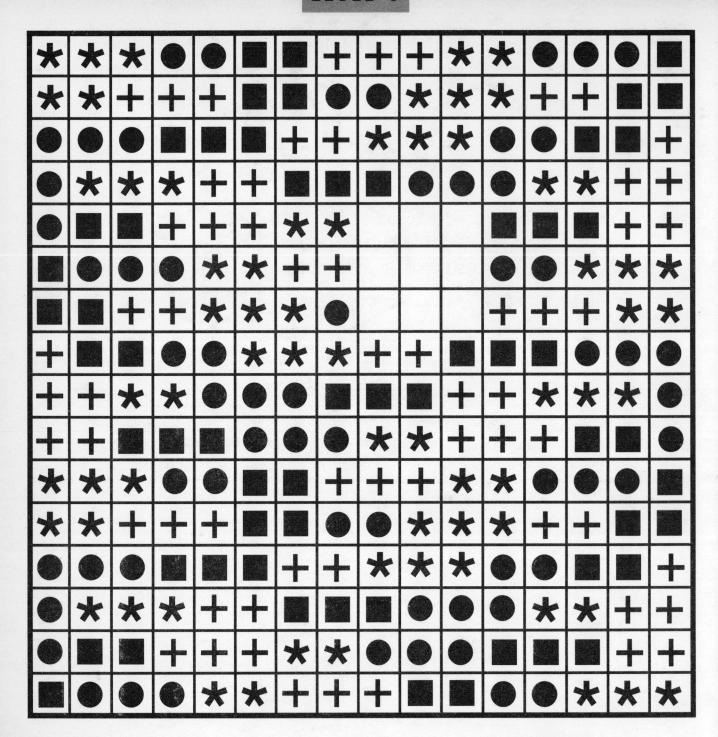

PUZZLE 135

The symbols in this grid behave in a predictable manner. When you have discovered their sequence it should be possible to fill in the blank segment.

See answer 11

D2 C4 A2 A5 D2 D4
C5 B4 A5 D2 D2 A5
C2 B4 A3 B3 A5 C1 C1 A5
E2 C4 C1 B1 B2 A1 C3 B2
A4 C4 C1 C4 D2 A5 D3
D3 B4 C3 A5 A1 A4
D2 A1 A3 B3 A5 C1
C2 A1 B2 C3 D5 D3

PUZZLE 136

This time the code is a little more difficult. To help you
we will give you a clue. The coded words are first names
from around the world.

See answer **139**

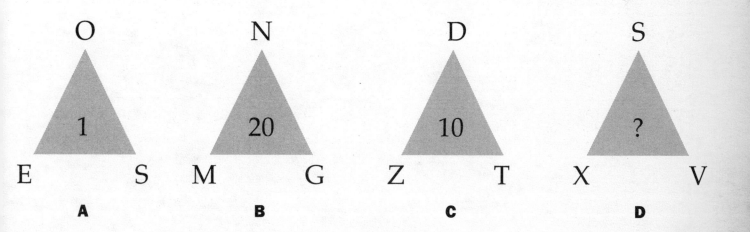

O   N   D   S

1   20   10   ?

E   S   M   G   Z   T   X   V

A   **B**   **C**   **D**

PUZZLE 137

Can you work out the rule these triangles follow and
find the missing number?

See answer **69**

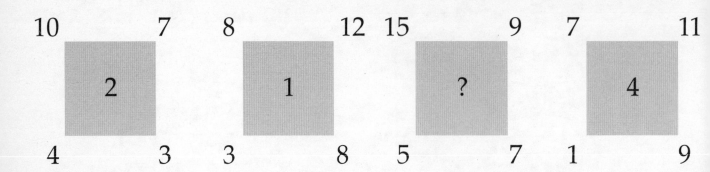

10	7	8	12	15	9	7	11
	2		1		?		4
4	3	3	8	5	7	1	9

PUZZLE 138

Can you work out which number should replace the
question mark in the square?

See answer 67

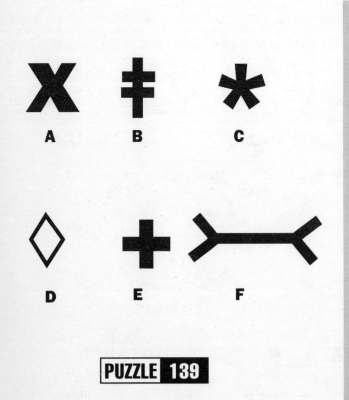

PUZZLE 139

Can you find the odd one out of these symbols?

See answer 120

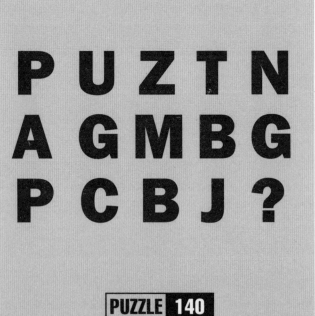

P U Z T N
A G M B G
P C B J ?

PUZZLE 140

Can you find the letter that should replace the
question mark?

See answer 50

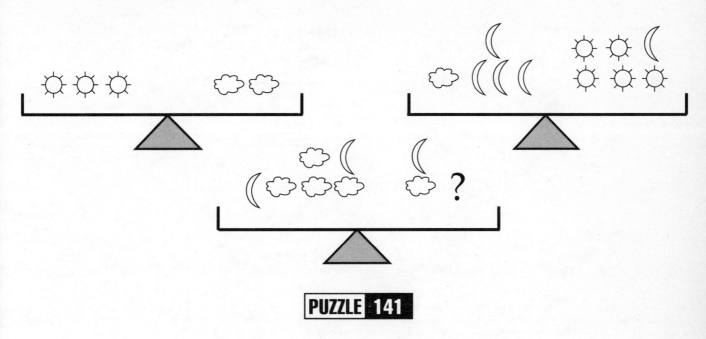

PUZZLE 141

Can you work out how many suns should replace the question mark, so that the scales balance?

See answer 73

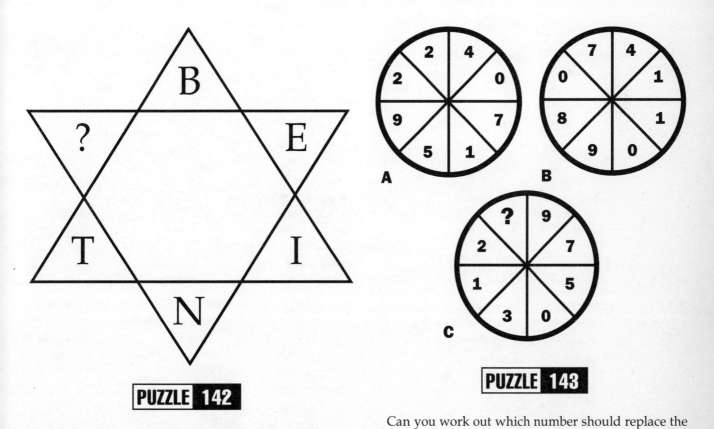

PUZZLE 142

PUZZLE 143

Can you find the letter that would complete the star?

See answer 91

Can you work out which number should replace the question mark to follow the rules of the other wheels?

See answer 32

Answer 1

A.	California	F.	Oregon
B.	Texas	G.	Virginia
C.	Nebraska	H.	Florida
D.	Alaska	I.	Colorado
E.	Idaho	J.	Arizona

Answer 2

C. The number in the middle is the sum of the squares of the numbers at the points of the triangles. C does not fit this pattern.

Answer 3.

B. The number of sides of the internal figures should increase by one each time. B is the odd one out because its internal figures should have 2 sides.

Answer 4

N. Multiply the two numbers in each segment. Their product is used to represent a letter (based on its numerical position in the alphabet). This letter is put in the segment diametrically opposite the original numbers.

Answer 5

One sun. The values are: Cloud = 3; Umbrella = 2; Moon = 4; Sun = 7.

Answer 6

$6 + 7 + 11 \div 3 \times 2 + 5 - 12 = 9$.

Answer 7

23. Square = 9; Cross = 5; Z = 6; Heart = 7.

Answer 8

E. Turn the diagram by 90° clockwise.

Answer 9

27. A number in the first circle is squared and the product is put in the corresponding segment of the second circle. The original number is then cubed and that product is put in the corresponding segment of the third circle.

Answer 10

$F - B + J - B = L$.

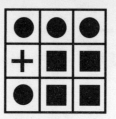

Answer 11

The pattern is a horizontal boustrophedon starting at the top left. The sequence is: 3 stars, 2 circles, 2, squares, 3 crosses, 2 stars, 3 circles, 3 squares, 2 crosses, etc.

Answer 12

E. It contains no curved lines.

Answer 13

B.and **H**.

Answer 14

4 moons. Sun = 9; Moon = 5; Cloud = 3.

Answer 15

E.

Answer 16

Q. The letters are in the following alphabetical order: miss one, miss two, miss three, miss one etc.

Answer 17

$4 \times 7 \div 2 + 8 + 9 \times 6 \div 3 = 62$.

Answer 18

B. The value of each letter in the alphabet is two-thirds of the number in the opposite segment.

Answer 19

10. Replace each letter by the value of its position in the alphabet. Start at E and add 1, then 2, then 3, then 4, then 5, then 1, then 2 etc. When you reach 26 (Z), go back to 1 (A).

Answer 20

6.20. The minute hand advances 20 minutes each time, the hour hand goes back 2 hours each time.

Answer 21

19. Starting from D, each number, or its alphabetic equivalent, advances three.

Answer 22
A. Letters represent values based on their position in the alphabet. In each column, subtract the letter in the middle row from the letter in the top row and place the answer in the bottom row.

Answer 23
33. Star = 8; Tick = 12; Cross = 13; Circle = 5.

Answer 24
2. The faces represent numbers, based on the elements in or around the face (excluding the head). Multiply the top number with the bottom right number and divide by the bottom left number. Place the answer in the middle.

Answer 25
A. Pattern is: 2 by arch on top, 4 by arch at right, 3 by arch on bottom, 2 by arch at left. Start at the top left corner and move down the grid in vertical lines, reverting to the top when of the next column when you reach the bottom.

Answer 26

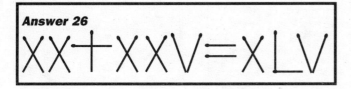

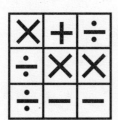

Answer 27
The order is 2 +, 3 −, 2 ÷, 3 x. The puzzle goes in an inward clockwise spiral starting from the top left corner.

Answer 28

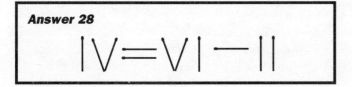

Answer 29
L. Add the value of the two letters in each outer segment, based on their position in the alphabet, and place the answer letter in the opposite inner segment.

Answer 30
R. Multiply the value of the three earliest letters, based on their value in the alphabet, by 2. The answer goes in the opposite tip. I (9) x 2 = 18 (R).

Answer 31
Five suns. Moons = 2; Cloud = 3; Sun = 4.

Answer 32
3. The numbers in each wheel add up to 30.

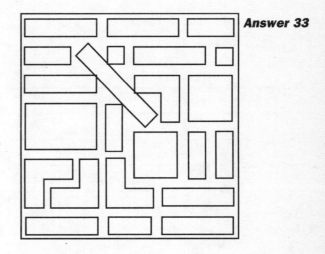

Answer 33

Answer 34
4. Imagine these are six-digit numbers. Add the bottom line to the middle line to get the top line.

Answer 35
8. Starting at H, and working clockwise, subtract the value of second letter, based on its value in the alphabet, from the value of the first letter, and put sum in following corner.

Answer 36
C.

Answer 37
Napoleon, Churchill, Truman, De Gaulle, Kennedy, Ho Chi Minh, Gandhi, Mandela.

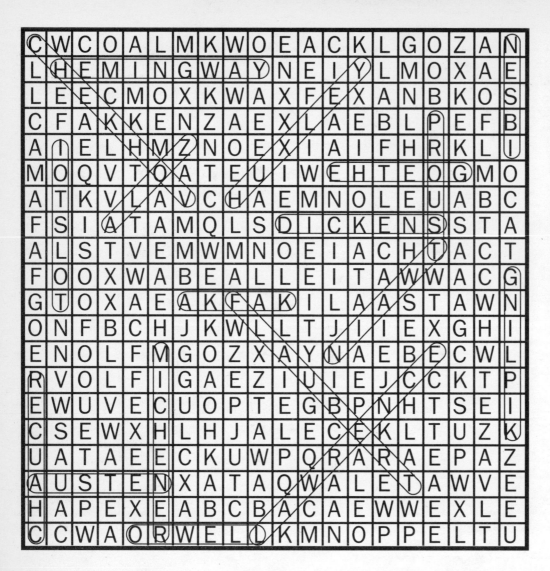

Answer 38

Austen
Hemingway
Michener
Chaucer
Huxley
Orwell
Chekov
Ibsen
Proust
Dickens
Kafka
Tolstoi
Flaubert
Kipling
Twain
Goethe
Lawrence
Zola

Answer 39

21. Add all the numbers of each triangle together and place the sum in the middle of next triangle. When you reach D put the sum in A.

Answer 40

The water in his garden was snow. He rolled several giant snowballs, built a pyramid and climbed onto the porch.

Answer 41

She was planting her mother's shoe tree.

Answer 42

Jim had moved from his home town years ago. He was watching the floods on the TV news. His wife had never liked the place anyway.

Answer 43

The old man had given them time. He left each of them the equivalent of their annual salary so that they could have a year to do what they liked.

Answer 44

This was a real bookworm, a bug that nibbles its way through books. Dr Gluck found him dining off his reference books.

Answer 45

Johnny wants to go through the glass tunnel at an aquarium.

Answer 46

Because three of them are on my wrist watch.

Answer 47

S. Look at opposite triangles. D is 4th letter of the alphabet, W is 4th from the end. F is 6th letter, while U is 6th from the end. H is the 8th letter, thus the missing letter is the one which is 8th from the end.

Answer 48

A.	Dallas	F.	Portland
B.	Seattle	G.	Detroit
C.	Chicago	H.	Atlanta
D.	Milwaukee	I.	Cincinnati
E.	Minneapolis	J.	Indianapolis

Answer 49

G. Add 2 elements to the body, take away 1, add 3, take away 2, add 4, take away 3.

Answer 50

B. In each column, divide the value of letter on the top row, based on its position in the alphabet, by the value of the second row letter to get the letter on the bottom row.

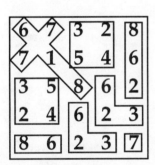

Answer 51

Answer 52

15. Start at the top left corner and add that number to each corner in a clockwise direction, eg. 7 + 7 = 14 + 7 = 21 + 7 = 28 + 7 = 35.

Answer 53

F + I + E – J + N – Y + H = I.

Answer 54

Whitehall, Trafalgar Square, Kensington Gardens, Marble Arch, Buckingham Palace, Piccadilly Circus, Grosvenor Square, Thames Embankment, Waterloo Station, Kings Cross.

Answer 55

72. Multiply all the numbers in the top sections to arrive at the number in the opposite bottom section. Multiply by 3 in the first circle, by 6 in the second one, and by 9 in the third circle.

Answer 56

825. Multiply the value of the letters, based on their value in the alphabet, from each triangle and place the product in the next but one triangle to the right.

Answer 57

A and **L**. The numbers are 3, 4, 6 and 9.

Answer 58

4. Multiply the two numbers in the outer circle of each spoke and place the product in the inner circle two spokes on in a clockwise direction.

Answer 59

35. Star = 6; Tick = 3; Cross = 17; Circle = 12.

Answer 60

Start at the top right corner and work in an inward spiral. The pattern is: two ticks, one heart, two faces, one tick, two hearts, one face, etc.

Answer 61 – See page 74

Answer 62

Arlington, Bethesda, Columbia Pike, Silver Spring, Mount Rainier, Chevy Chase, Georgetown, Anacostia. U = A, Z = F, A = G, T = Z, etc.

Answer 63

16. Add 2, subtract 1, add 4, subtract 2, add 8, subtract 4, add 16, subtract 8.

Answer 64

6.50. The minute hand moves back 5, 10 and 15 minutes, while the hour hand moves forward 1, 2 and 3 hours.

```
P B A W N W O C H K T V E N T A C Y X O
A A D E F W O Y J U L I A R O B E R T S
C O U S T I N H O F F M A N B R M O N L
K A O L W O L N N Y G O R E S O T U V D
K M G E N E W I L D E R W O L O Z B R R
C A S K L E M U O T L B W J L K K E G O
P C M W V U W E A I J L G A H E T E B F
E L K E F O Z M A A T H E N A S E R O D
E S O A L L A M A A O I E E O H I L L E
R T A S E G F A A N T O E F L I S T R R
T O M C R U I S E S R S E O T E E E P T
S A O E E B W B I M Q I A N E L G N O R
L A A O H E H R S T D A B D C D O A T E
Y A F G S V H T E Q I B K A R S C E J B
R B P O A C F A J Z N A Y A A Y I X Q O
E N O Z E A L M A O C Y H F O G H E L R
M A E I N A Z E N I A C L E A H C I M B
C P L M A N N V W X I E R S F L A Z O N
N U W M J F G Q S R A E L L A E S S O E
J O N Y F G I N O S P M O H T A M M E F
```

Answer 65
D.

Answer 66
Bois de Boulogne, Montparnasse, Madeleine, Pere Lachaise, Champs Elysees, Gare de Lyon, Arc de Triomphe, Montmartre. The code here is: I = A, Z = R, A = S, H = Z, etc.

Answer 67
8. Subtract the bottom left corner from the top left corner. Now subtract the bottom right corner from the top right corner, then subtract this answer from the first difference and put the number in the middle.

Answer 68 – See opposite page

Answer 69
21. Find the value of each letter based on its position in the alphabet, then add the values of the top and left corner together. Subtract the bottom right corner from this number and place the new value in the middle of the triangle.

Answer 70
Q. Reading clockwise from the top, numbers correspond to the alphabetic position of the following letter.

Answer 71
16. All the other numbers can be divided by 3.

Answer 72
M X O. The first line values of letters, based on their position in the alphabet, increase by 3. The

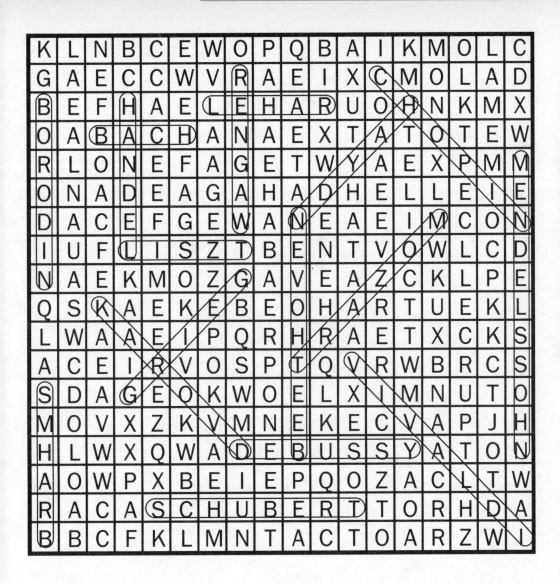

Answer 68

- Bach
- Dvorak
- Mendelssohn
- Beethoven
- Grieg
- Mozart
- Borodin
- Handel
- Purcell
- Brahms
- Haydn
- Schubert
- Chopin
- Lehar
- Vivaldi
- Debussy
- Liszt
- Wagner

second line values increase by 4 and the third line values increase by 5.

Answer 73

Six suns. Values are: Sun = 6; Moon = 7; Cloud = 9.

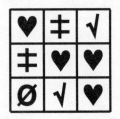

Answer 74

Start at top left corner and move in a vertical boustrophedon. The order is two hearts, one square root, two crossed circles, one cross, one heart, two square roots, one crossed circle, two crosses, etc.

Answer 75

Little Italy, Greenwich Village, Manhattan, Times Square, Gramercy Park, Soho, Central Park, Chinatown.

Answer 76

Go first along the top of the triangles, then along the bottoms. Each circle is filled one quarter more until the circle is complete, then reverts to one quarter filled.

Answer 77

4	4	5	6	7	8	9	0
4	3	2	4	5	6	2	3
5	2	6	2	4	0	0	9

| 6 | 4 | 2 | 8 | 9 | 4 | 5 | 2 |
| 7 | 5 | 4 | 9 | 7 | 7 | 8 | 9 |

8	6	0	4	7	3	2	5
9	2	0	5	8	2	3	6
0	3	9	2	9	5	6	4

Answer 78
40. Star = 7; Tick = 8; Cross = 14; Circle = 11.

Answer 79
Copenhagen, Prague, London, Berlin, Tokyo, Amsterdam, Stockholm, Colombo, Madrid, Ankara.

Answer 80
42. Take the number in the middle of the square, divide it by the number in the top left corner and place the new number in the bottom right corner. Again take the middle number, but now divide it by the number in the top right corner and place this new number in the bottom left corner.

Answer 81
55. Add the two last numbers together.

Answer 82
E and **O**. The letters are N, O, P and X.

Answer 83
1.00. The minute hand moves forward 20 minutes, the hour hand moves back 1 hour.

Answer 84
B. Start from top left corner and move in a vertical boustrephedon. Order is: 4 smiley face, 1 sad face, 3 straight mouth, 2 face with hair, etc.

Answer 85

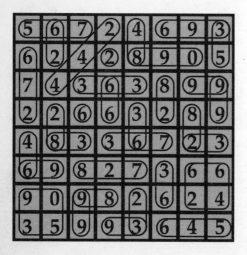

Answer 86
Z. Take the value of the letters, based on their position in the alphabet. A back 3 is X; X forward 4 is B; B back 3 is Y; Y forward 4 is C, etc.

Answer 87
7. Add the three numbers at the corner of each triangle, multiply by 2 and place that number in the middle.

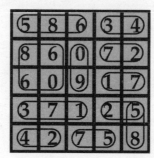

Answer 88

Answer 89
Top half: **÷ x**; bottom half: **x x**.

Answer 90
A. Add one new element to the face, then add one hair and an element to the face, then a hair, then a hair and an element to the face, repeat sequence.

Answer 91
A. Based on the alphabet, starting at B miss 2 letters, then 3, then 4, etc.

Answer 92
A.	Manchester	F.	Bangkok
B.	Glasgow	G.	Calcutta
C.	Toulouse	H.	Melbourne
D.	Smolensk	I.	Barcelona
E.	Vancouver	J.	Sacramento

Answer 93 – See opposite page

Answer 94
39. Star = 9; Tick = 6; Cross =3; Circle = 24.

Answer 95
Piccadilly, Copacabana, Guggenheim, Etoile, Whitehall, Madeleine, Central Park, Colosseum.

Answer 93

Arafat
Gandhi
Mussolini
Ben Gurion
Gorbachev
Napoleon
Bismarck
Kennedy
Pinochet
Churchill
Lincoln
Stalin
De Gaulle
MaoTse Tung
Thatcher
Franco
Mitterand
Yeltsin

Answer 96
One arrow pointing up.

Answer 97
14. Multiply the number on the left of the triangle by the number on top, take away the number on the right from this product and put this number in the middle.

Answer 98
68. Square = 7; X = 11; Z = 3; Heart = 17.

Answer 99
I and **K**. The figures are: matchstick man, triangle, half-moon, circle, stile.

Answer 100
6.45. The minute hand moves back 15, 30 and 45 minutes. The hour hand moves forward 3, 6 and 9 hours.

Answer 101
A diamond.

Answer 102
B, F and **N**.

Answer 103
F. The numbers made up of odd numbers are reversed.

Answer 104
4. The number relates to the number of shapes in which the number is enclosed.

Answer 105
Chicago, Kansas, Houston, Birmingham, Detroit, Atlanta, Phoenix, Memphis.

Answer 106
27. 2 + 3 = 5 + 4 = 9 + 5 = 14 + 6 = 20 + 7 = 27.

Answer 107
E and **I**.

Answer 108
– – X.

Answer 109
Elton John, Freddie Mercury, Lisa Stansfield, Sinead O'Connor, Meatloaf, Madonna, Michael Jackson, Rod Stewart. A = J, Z = I.

Answer 110
D. The large letter turns 90° clockwise, the small letter turns 180°.

Answer 111
26. The digits in each of the other balls add up to 10.

Answer 112
2. Relates to the number of shapes which enclose each figure.

Answer 113
Oregon, Nebraska, Nevada, Wisconsin, Florida, Virginia, Texas, Colorado.

Answer 114
Chekhov, Brecht, Wilde, Beckett, Genet, Goethe, Ibsen, Racine.

Answer 115
Picasso, Rembrandt, Gaugin, Leonardo, Constable, Raphael, Van Gogh, Matisse. A = 1:4; B = 1:3; C = 1:2; D = 1:1; E = 2:4, etc.

Answer 116
D. Letters with only curves stay the same, letters with curves and straight lines turn by 90° and letters with only straight lines by 180°.

Answer 117
Top half: **X ÷**; bottom half: **÷ X**.

Answer 118
31. In all the other numbers the first digit is smaller than the second one.

Answer 119
Gazpacho, Mulligatawny, Borscht, Minestrone, Chowder, Avgolemono, Cock-a-Leekie, Bouillabaisse. A = 1, Z = 26.

Answer 120
The diamond. It is a closed shape.

Answer 121
G. The internal patterns are reversed.

Answer 122
15. All the other numbers have not got a divisor.

Answer 123
Vivaldi, Beethoven, Grieg, Bizet, Mahler, Wagner, Mozart, Elgar.

Answer 124
3. The numbers refer to the number of shapes which surround each digit.

Answer 125
K and **O**.

Answer 126
Top half: **+ +**; bottom half: **+ –**.

Answer 127
F. The symbols are reflected over a vertical line.

Answer 128
Heathrow, Fort Worth, Ben Gurion, Las Palmas, O'Hare, Gatwick, Haneda, Shannon. A = R; B = S, etc.

Answer 129
$5 \times 4 \div 2 + 7 = 17$.

Answer 130
D and **L**.

Answer 131
C. The letters represent values based on their position in the alphabet. They represent the number of straight-sided figures in which they are enclosed. The circle is a red herring.

Answer 132
Julia Roberts, Burt Reynolds, Jack Nicholson, David Niven, Marilyn Monroe, Jeremy Irons, Audrey Hepburn, Winona Ryder.

Answer 133
K. Only the K has serifs.

Answer 134
C and **K**.

Answer 135
Coq au vin, Paella, Dim sum, Sushi, Bratwurst, Hamburger, Spaghetti, Vindaloo. A = 20, B = 21.

Answer 136
Top half: **+ −**; bottom half: **− −**.

Answer 137
C. It has an odd number of elements, the others all have an even number.

Answer 138
C. In the others the small shapes added together result in the large shape.

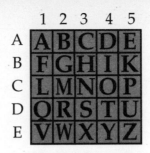

Answer 139
Robert, Pierre, Michelle, Wolfgang, Dolores, Sinead, Rachel, Magnus.

Answer 140
C. The symbol consists of 3 parts, the others only of 2.

Answer 141
Asimov, Balzac, Hemingway, Joyce, Maugham, Miller, Proust, Twain.

Answer 142
E and **M**.

Answer 143
$M − E + B + D = N$.

GARGANTUA MIND MAZE

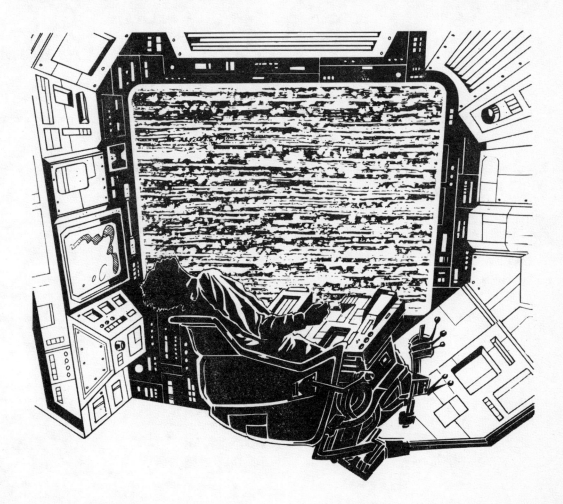

GARGANTUA, the super-computer that controls communications and transport in most of the developed world, has gone haywire. Dr Ben Eischrank, the computer's inventor and guardian, was carrying out routine maintenance when a freak electric shock hit him. Now the world is plunged into chaos. Only you, Eischrank's trusted assistant, can restore the computer to normality. But there is a problem. The doctor was so insanely jealous of anyone touching his invention that he guarded it with a fiendishly intricate system of enigmas to prevent unauthorized access.

Can you penetrate this mental maze and save the world? The solution to each puzzle will tell which you should tackle next. When you have worked your way around the maze you will receive a code number which allows access to the computer. But hurry, for as you work a video screen on the laboratory wall shows the devastation which is sweeping the earth. Planes plunge from the sky, whole cities are blacked out, panic and devastation are spreading like the plague. Don't delay, begin now! It is vital that you write down the number of every puzzle you complete in the order in which you complete it.

Five boys are going to visit relatives. Tom goes to Georgia, Sid goes to Hawaii, William goes to Dakota, and Orville goes to Louisiana. Does George go to

A) Wyoming
B) California
C) Tennessee
D) Oregon
E) Alaska?

If you choose A, go to 22.
If you choose B, go to 11.
If you choose C, go to 7.
If you choose D, go to 16.
If you choose E, go to 10.

PUZZLE 1

See answer 1

Below are seven 6-digit numbers all of which can be divided by 136 with no remainder. They all begin with 117 but the other digits have been concealed. Can you work out what they are? When you have done so, add together the final digits of all seven numbers, subtract 2 and go to the puzzle indicated.

	???
	???
117	**???**
	???
	???
	???
	???

PUZZLE 2

See answer 2

This diagram represents a treasure map. The treasure is under the square marked with an asterisk. You are allowed to stop on each square only once (though you may cross a square as often as you like). When you stop on a square you must follow the instructions you find there. The letters stand for points of the compass

N = North; S = South; E = East; W = West

and the numbers stand for the number of squares you must travel (e.g. a square marked 3SW would instruct you to move three squares South West). In order to find the treasure which square would you start on? When you have the co-ordinate (one letter and one number) add 15 to the number and go to the corresponding puzzle.

A	B	C	D	E	F	G	H	
2E	2SE	3S	4E	1S	1SE	4S	1W	**1**
1SE	1N	3S	3W	3W	2S	1S	2S	**2**
4E	4E	4S	3SW	2S	3S	1NW	1N	**3**
3NE	2SE	3NE	1NW	2NW	4W	2W	3NW	**4**
4N	1S	2NW	2W	3SW	2NE	2SW	1SW	**5**
2S	1SW	2NW	4N	3E	2SE	2S	1S	**6**
3E	✳	3E	3N	3W	1S	3N	2NW	**7**
3E	3E	2N	3NW	2N	1NE	4W	3N	**8**

PUZZLE 3

See answer 3

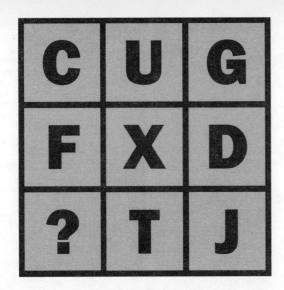

Look at the grid. Can you discover the logic used in its construction? When you have done so you will be able to replace the question mark with a letter. If you choose B, go to 35. If you choose H, go to 23. If you choose J, go to 17.

See answer **4**

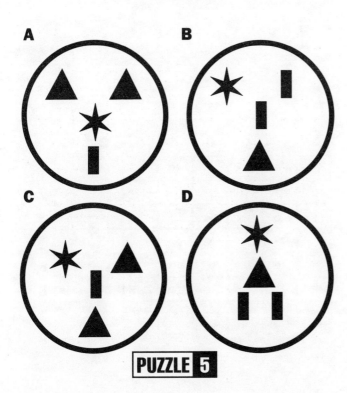

PUZZLE 5

Find the odd one out. If you choose A, go to 14. If you choose B, go to 17. If you choose C, go to 20. If you choose D, go to 15.

See answer **5**

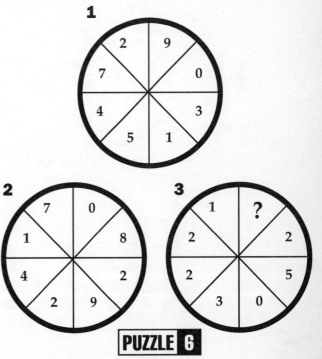

PUZZLE 6

Which number replaces the question mark? Add 24 and go to a new puzzle.

See answer **6**

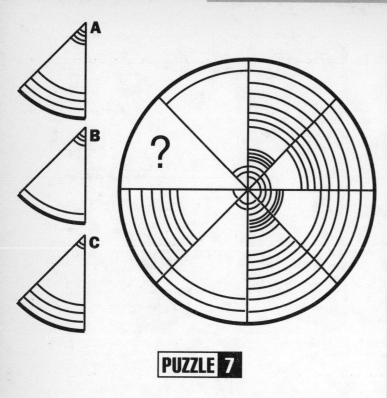

PUZZLE 7

Which sector correctly fills the blank? If you choose A, go to 10. If you choose B, go to 13. If you choose C, go to 34.

See answer 7

Pizza	$2.90
Frankfurters	$6.60
Lasagne	$4.10
Chilli con Carne	$8.00
Moussaka	$4.80

PUZZLE 8

Al's Diner has a unique menu. Al has his own special way of calculating his prices. Can you work out what it is and discover what he charges for Doner Kebab? Add the digits in that number, add 17 and go to the next puzzle.

See answer 8

The diagram on the right represents a treasure map. The treasure lies under the square with an asterisk. You are allowed to stop on each square only once (though you may cross a square as often as you like). When you stop on a square you must follow the instructions you find there. The letters stand for points of the compass

N = North; S = South; E = East; W = West

and the numbers for the number of squares you must travel (e.g. a square marked 3SW would instruct you to move three squares South West). Which is the starting square? When you have the co-ordinates 12 to the digit and go to the puzzle of that number.

A	B	C	D	E	F	G	H	
2S	1SE	2W	3S	4S	2W	1SE	3W	**1**
4E	2E	2SW	2SW	2S	1E	1S	4S	**2**
1NE	4S	3S	2W	2W	*	4S	2NW	**3**
1SE	4S	1NE	3NE	3SE	3W	1SE	3N	**4**
3N	1S	4N	2NE	3SE	3N	2NW	1SW	**5**
4E	2E	2SW	2NE	1NE	2NE	2S	2SW	**6**
2NE	1SE	2NW	4NE	1W	1N	3N	2W	**7**
1N	1NE	2NW	3N	1N	2W	3N	3W	**8**

PUZZLE 9

See answer 9

1

2

3

PUZZLE 10

Can you work out the logic of this diagram and replace the question mark with a number? When you have the correct number subtract 45 and go to the puzzle of that number.

See answer 10

10	L		I	12
O				Z
M				B
?	N		D	10

PUZZLE 11

Look at the grid and work out what should go in place of the question mark? Subtract 5 and go to the puzzle whose number you now have.

See answer 11

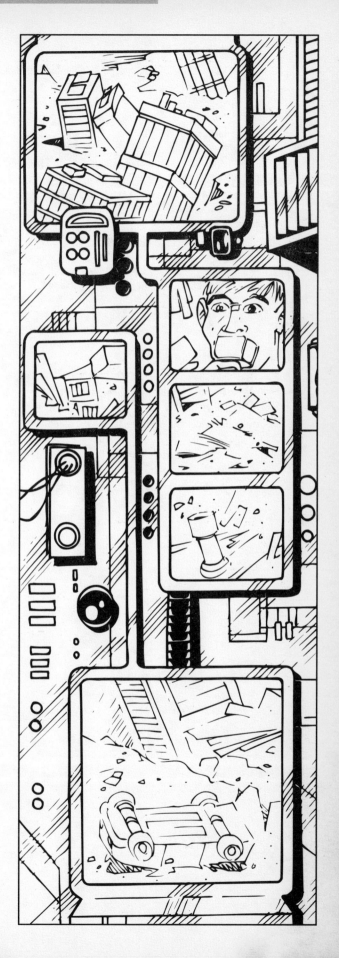

PUZZLE 12

The shapes in this grid appear in a set order. Work out what that order is and fill in the last square. If you choose Diamond, go to 16. If you choose Circle, go to 5. If you choose Heart, go to 13. If you choose Triangle, go to 17. If you choose Moon, go to 10.

See answer 12

PUZZLE 13

These clock faces follow a pattern. Can you work out what the second clock face should look like? Add the number indicated by the hour hand to the number indicated by the minute hand, add 12 to that sum and go to the puzzle indicated.

See answer 13

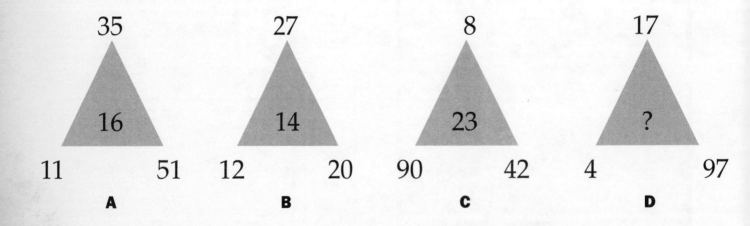

35	27	8	17
16	14	23	?
11 51	12 20	90 42	4 97
A	**B**	**C**	**D**

PUZZLE 14

Find a number to replace the question mark in Triangle D. Add 6 to your answer and go to that puzzle.

See answer 14

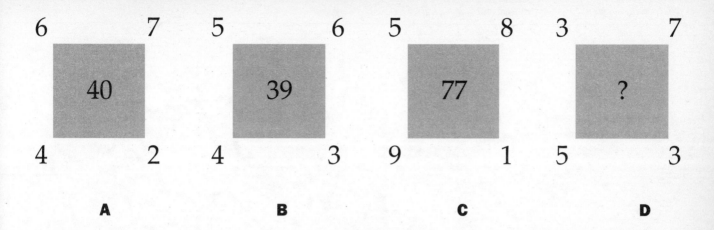

PUZZLE 15

Can you work out which number should replace the question mark in the last square? When you have the number subtract 36 and go to the next puzzle.

See answer 15

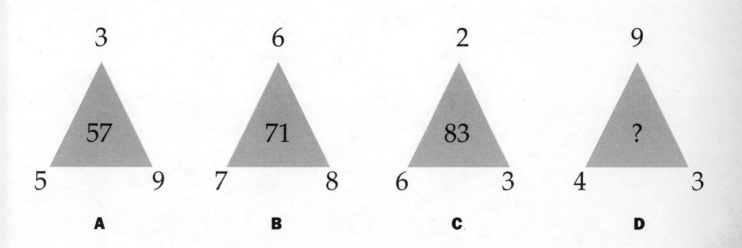

PUZZLE 16

Can you work out which number should replace the question mark? When you have the number subtract 21 and go to the puzzle of the resulting number.

See answer 16

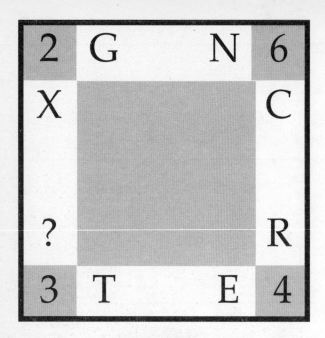

PUZZLE 17

This square follows a certain pattern. Can you work it out and replace the question mark with a letter? If you choose M, go to 16. If you choose D, go to 30. If you choose H, go to 27. If you choose F, go to 2.

See answer 17

PUZZLE 18

Can you crack the reasoning behind this spider's web and find the missing letter? If you choose Z, go to 31. If you choose V, go to 23. If you choose M, go to 13.

See answer 18

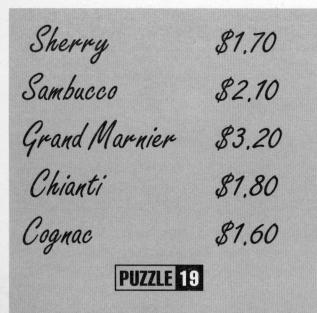

Sherry	$1.70
Sambucco	$2.10
Grand Marnier	$3.20
Chianti	$1.80
Cognac	$1.60

PUZZLE 19

In Maria's Bar the prices for drinks are calculated in an unusual way. Can you work it out and find out the price Maria charges for Whiskey? When you have the price discard the dollars and subtract 66 from the remaining cents.
You will then have the number of the next puzzle.

See answer 19

Five boys travel abroad by ship. Andy boards the *Elizabeth II*, John travels on the *Norway*, Peter sails on the *Tasmania*, Nick chooses the *Rover*. Which ship does Larry board?

A) Enterprise
B) Sea Sprite
C) Panama
D) Neptune
E) Iolanthe

If you choose A, go to 19.
If you choose B, go to 6.
If you choose C, go to 32.
If you choose D, go to 28.
If you choose E, go to 5.

PUZZLE 20

See answer 20

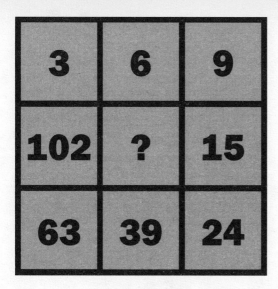

3	6	9
102	?	15
63	39	24

PUZZLE 21

Can you work out the logic of this square and find the missing number? When you have your answer subtract 163 and go to the puzzle of that number.

See answer 21

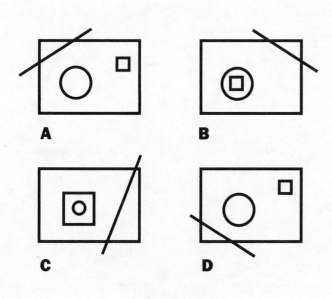

A   B

C   D

PUZZLE 22

Which of the above diagrams does not follow the same rule as the others? If you choose A, go to 17. If you choose B, go to 6. If you choose C, go to 29. If you choose D, go to 30.

See answer 22

PUZZLE 23

Each of the following girls has to work on a project about a famous statesman. Yvonne chooses Bismarck, Henrietta chooses Stalin, Trudie decides to work on Gandhi, Irene picks Roosevelt and Virginia chooses Eisenhower. Who of the following does Natasha choose:

a) **Churchill**
b) **Mao**
c) **Charlemagne**
d) **Reagan**
e) **Sadat**

If you think the answer is A, go to 6.
If B, go to 19. If C, go to 31.
If D, go to 34. If E, go to 15.

See answer 23

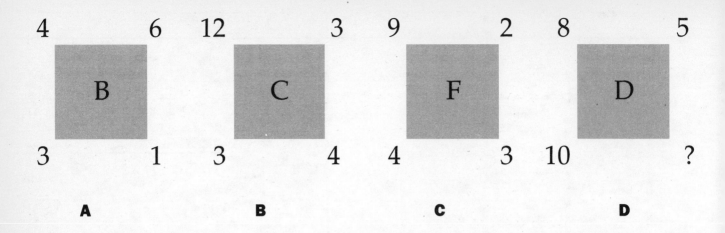

4	6	12	3	9	2	8	5
B		C		F		D	
3	1	3	4	4	3	10	?

A   B   C   D

PUZZLE 24

Can you find the number which should replace the
question mark? When you have it add 2 and go to
the next puzzle.

See answer 24

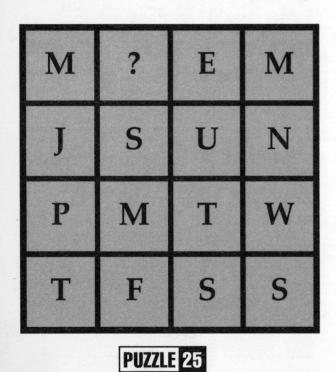

M	?	E	M
J	S	U	N
P	M	T	W
T	F	S	S

PUZZLE 25

Look at the diagram and replace the question mark
with a letter. When you have the answer convert the
letter into a number by using its position in the
alphabetical order (A=1, B=2... Z=26), subtract five
and then go to the puzzle of that number.

See answer 25

PUZZLE 26

Can you find out which letter should replace the
question mark in this spider's web?
If your answer is K, go to 29. If you choose U,
go to 18. If your answer is G, go to 7.

See answer 26

This is the end of the Mind Maze.
To find the code that will allow
you to access Gargantua you
must add up the numbers of all
the puzzles on your route between
puzzles 16 and 23 inclusive.
The sum of these numbers
will give you the code.

PUZZLE 27

See answer 27

```
        ???
        ???
115     ???
        ???
        ???
        ???
```

PUZZLE 28

Above are six 6-digit numbers each beginning
with 115. All the numbers are divisible by 173 with
no remainder. Which digits do you need to complete
the numbers? Add the last digits of all six numbers
together, add 8 and go to the puzzle whose
number you now have.

See answer 28

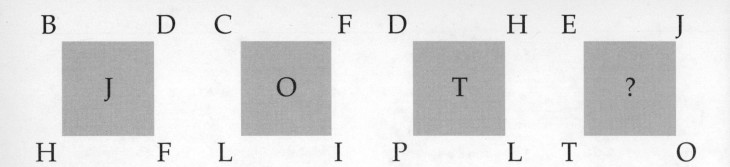

B D C F D H E J

J O T ?

H F L I P L T O

PUZZLE 29

Can you work out the logic behind the letters on these squares and find the one that should replace the question mark? If you choose F, go to 29. If you choose K, go to 16. If you choose Y, go to 3.

See answer 29

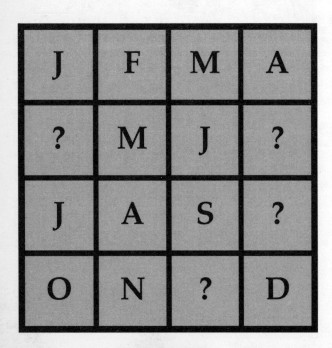

J	F	M	A
?	M	J	?
J	A	S	?
O	N	?	D

PUZZLE 30

The question marks in this grid have a numerical significance. In fact they are all related to the same number. When you know what that number is, subtract 7 and go to the next puzzle.

See answer 30

PUZZLE 31

This diagram represents a treasure map. The treasure lies under the square marked with an asterisk. You are allowed to stop on each square only once (though you may cross a square as often as you like). When you stop on a square you must follow the instructions you find there. The letters stand for points of the compass

N = North, S = South, E = East, W = West

and the numbers stand for the number of squares you must travel (e.g. a square marked 3SW would instruct you to move three squares South West). In order to find the treasure which square would you start on? When you have the co-ordinate, add 10 to the digit and go to the next puzzle.

See answer 31

	A	B	C	D	E	F	G	H	
	2SE	4E	1S	1S	2W	1SW	1SE	4W	**1**
	2S	1SW	1SE	2SW	2SE	4S	3S	2SW	**2**
	1N	2N	3S	4SE	2SW	2E	1NW	1NW	**3**
	2E	*	3S	3NE	3S	4S	4S	3NW	**4**
	4N	4E	1W	2NW	2N	1SE	3W	4N	**5**
	2SE	4N	2SE	2W	4W	2NE	2NW	2S	**6**
	3E	1S	1W	3N	2E	4N	4N	2W	**7**
	1N	3NE	2W	3NW	3NE	2NE	2NW	4W	**8**

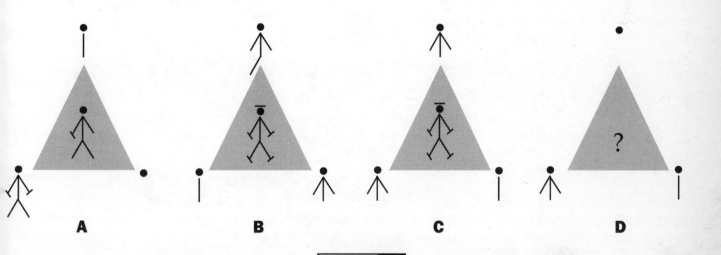

A   **B**   **C**   **D**

PUZZLE 32

Can you work out what the matchstick man in the middle of the last triangle should look like? Take the number of elements in the matchstick man, add 4 and go to the next puzzle.

See answer 32

Each of the following girls have to name their favourite pop group.

Jessica's is Genesis, Elspeth's is Bon Jovi, Zoe's is Wet Wet Wet, Patricia's is Meatloaf and Gwendoline's favourite band is Dire Straits. Which of these girls chooses Queen? A) Annabelle B) Roberta C) Barbara D) Dolly E) Trixie.

If you choose A, go to 8.
If you choose B, go to 32.
If you choose C, go to 26.
If you choose D, go to 3.
If you choose E, go to 21.

PUZZLE 33

See answer 33

```
     ???
     ???
124  ???
     ???
     ???
     ???
```

PUZZLE 34

Above are six 6-digit numbers each beginning with the numbers 124. Each of the numbers is divisible by 149 with no remainder. Which digits do you need to complete the numbers? Add all the last digits together, subtract 16 and go to the next puzzle.

See answer 34

PUZZLE 35

Can you work out the sequence of this snake and find the missing shape. If you choose Diamond, go to 12. If you choose Heart, go to 16. If you choose Cross, go to 9. If you choose Circle, go to 17. If you choose Arrow, go to 3.

See answer 35

Answer 1
C, go to 7. G (the first letter of George) is the 7th letter from the beginning of the alphabet, T (for Tennessee) is 7th from the end.

Answer 2
117096, 117232, 117368, 117504, 117640, 117776 117912. Divide 117000 by 136. Round the number up to the next full number, then multiply it by 136, then keep adding 136 to this number.
6 + 2 + 8 + 4 + 0 + 6 + 2 = 28. 28 − 2 = 26.

Answer 3
D5. Work backward from the ✳ (Finish) square.
5+15=20.

Answer 4
B, go to 35. The letters represent numbers based on their position in the alphabet. Those in the left column and multiplied by those in the right to give the letters in the middle.

Answer 5
D, go to 15. The diagrams make "faces", D is upside down.

Answer 6
1. The corresponding sections of the three wheels add up to 10. 1 + 24 = 25.

Answer 7
A, go to 10. The outer lines of one sector added to the inner lines of the sector opposite always add up to 9.

Answer 8
$5.80. Vowels = 7, Consonants = 5. 5 + 8 + 17 = 30.

Answer 9
B1. Work back from the ✳ (Finish) square. 1 + 12 = 13.

Answer 10
73. Starting at 1 add 5, then 4, then 3, then 2, then 1, and repeat order. When you arrive at the highest number move on to the lowest number in the next wheel. 73 − 45 = 28.

Answer 11
9. Take the value of each letter, add their digits together and put number in space to the right.
9 − 5 = 4.

Answer 12
Circle, go to 5. The basic sequence is Heart, Circle, Diamond, Triangle, Moon. Take the first symbol and put a line through it. The rest of the sequence then repeats in reverse order. Repeat this with each symbol in turn.

Answer 13
4.30. The numbers are divided by 2 on each clock.
4 + 6 + 12 = 22.

Answer 14
28. Add individual digits of each number on edge of triangle and place their sum in the middle. 28 + 6 = 34

Answer 15
44. Multiply the diagonals of each square, then add both values together and put this number in the middle. 44 − 36 = 8.

Answer 16
30. Multiply the numbers at the bottom of each triangle, reverse the digits in the answer and add number on top of triangle. This number goes in the middle. 30 − 21 = 9.

Answer 17
H, go to 27. Start at top left hand corner, multiply number by value of following letter (based on its position in the alphabet), find new letter equivalent to that value and place in next space.

Answer 18
Z, go to 31. Subtract inner letter from outer, based on their position in the alphabet. The result of each calculation is 3.

Answer 19
$1.90. Vowel = 2, consonant = 3. Add all values together and multiply by 10. 90 − 66 = 24.

Answer 20
C, go to 32. The initial letter of each ship is four places down the alphabetical order from the initial letter of the boy's name.

Answer 21
165. 3 + 6 = 9, 6 + 9 = 15, 9 + 15 = 24, 15 + 24 = 39, 24 + 39 = 63, 39 + 63 = 102, 102 + 63 =165. 165 – 163 = 2.

Answer 22
C, go to 29. The line should cut off a triangle at one corner.

Answer 23
B, go to 19. In each pair, the girl's initial and the statesman's is the same number of letters from either the beginning or the end of the alphabet. Natasha, 13 letters from the end, studies Mao, 13 from the beginning.

Answer 24
4. Multiply the numbers on each left side and each right side of the square and divide the new value on the left by the new value on the right. 4 + 2 = 6.

Answer 25
V, go to 17. The letters are the initials of the planets in the solar system, followed by the days of the week. The order is a horizontal boustrophedon, starting from top left. Venus is missing, so V (22nd letter) – 5 = 17.

Answer 26
U, go to 18. Based on their position in the alphabet the inner letter is four places behind the outer letter.

Answer 27
The code number to access Gargantua is 335.

Answer 28
115045, 115218, 115391, 115564, 115737, 115910. Divide 115000 by 173 and round the answer up to the nearest whole number. Now multiply this number by 173 and add 173 to it until you reach 115910.
5 + 8 + 1 + 4 + 7 + 0 = 25. 25 + 8 = 33.

Answer 29
Y, go to 3. Based on the letters position in the alphabet and starting at the top left hand corner, in the first square add 2 to each value, in the second square add 3, in the third square add 4 and in the fourth square add 5.

Answer 30
17 + 6 =23. All the digits from 1-9 are represented as both tens and units. 1 is never used as a ten and 7 is never used as a unit.

Answer 31
D6. Work back from the ✳ (Finish) square. 6 + 10 = 16.

Answer 32
He should have 10 elements. Add the elements of matchstick men on each side of triangle and place new figure in middle of following triangle. Put figure based on corners of last triangle in middle of first triangle. 10 + 4 = 14.

Answer 33
E, go to 21. The initial letter of the girls name is three places ahead in the alphabet to the initial letter in the groups name.

Answer 34
124117, 124266 124415, 124564, 124713, 124862. Divide 124000 by 149 and round the answer up to the nearest whole number. Now multiply this number by 149 and add 149 to it until you reach 124862.
7 + 6 + 5 + 4 + 3 + 2 = 27. 27 – 16 = 11.

Answer 35
Diamond, go to 12. The sequence is Heart, Cross, Circle, Arrow, Diamond. Repeat sequence omitting the first symbol, then add first symbol with extra line around. Repeat with each symbol.

ORDER IS

1	7	10	28	33	21			
2	26	18	31	16	9	13	22	
29	3	20	32	14	34	11	4	35
12	5	15	8	30	23	19	24	6
25	17	27						

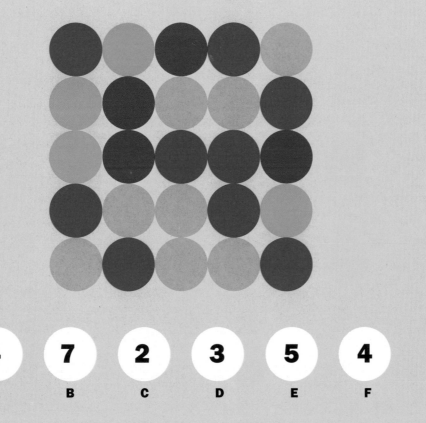

4	7	2	3	5	4
A	B	C	D	E	F

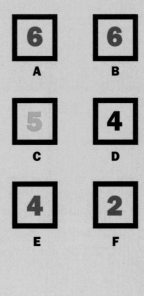

F	5	1	3	3	5
5	4	2	1	3	1
1	2	2	1	2	1
1	1	3	1	3	1
2	3	2	2	1	1
4	2	3	1	4	1
2	2	1	2	1	6

6	6
A	B

5	4
C	D

4	2
E	F

RAINBOW TEST

□ Pale Blue
■ Dark Blue
■ Pink
□ Orange
■ Green
■ Red
□ Yellow

1 Move from circle to touching circle, starting from the bottom left corner and finishing in the top right corner. Collect nine circles each time. How many different routes are there to collect four orange, three blue, one pink and one green?

2 Here is an unusual safe. Each of the buttons must be pressed only once in the correct order to open it. The last button is marked F. The number of moves is marked on each button. A black number means move down. A red number means move up. A pink number means move left and a green number means move right. Thus a red 1 would mean one move up, whilst a green 1 would mean one move to the right. Which button is the first you must press?

COLOUR TEST time limit 1 hour

RAINBOW TEST

3 Which circle is missing from this series?

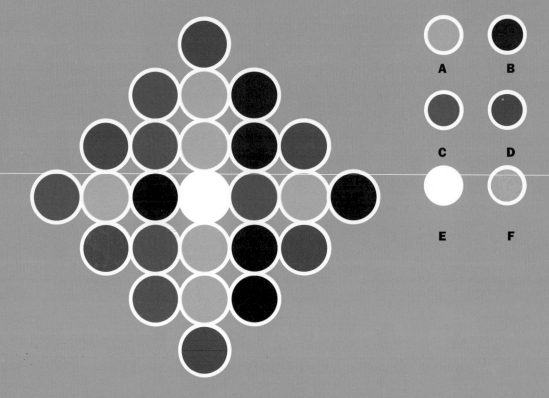

4 Which of the constructed boxes cannot be made from the pattern?

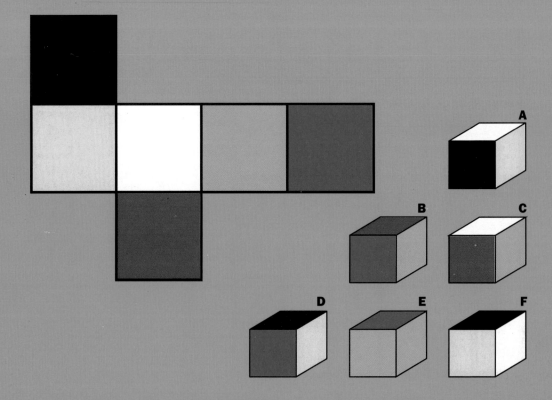

COLOUR TEST time limit 1 hour

RAINBOW TEST

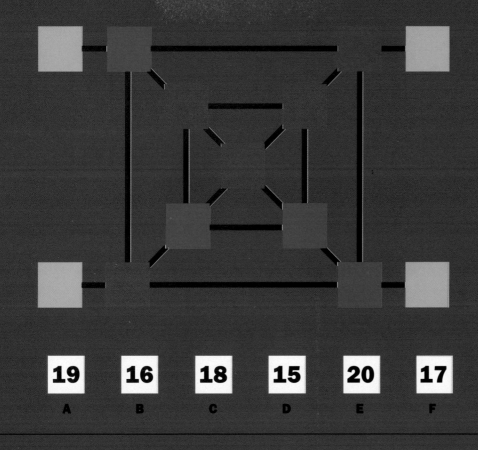

19	16	18	15	20	17
A	B	C	D	E	F

5 Start at any corner and follow the lines. Collect another four boxes. Green boxes are worth 2 each, red boxes are worth 4 and blue boxes are worth 3. Total the five boxes. What is the highest possible total?

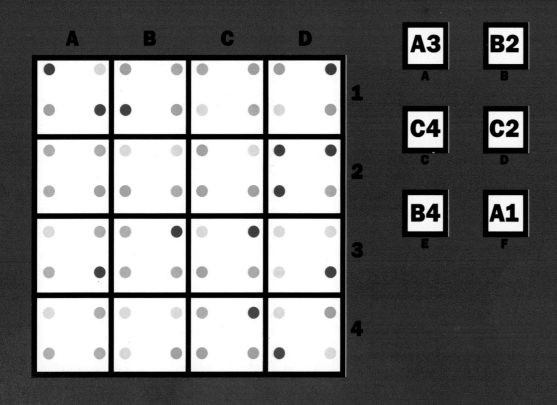

	A	B	C	D

1

2

3

4

A3	B2
A	B

C4	C2
C	D

B4	A1
E	F

6 Which square's contents matches B1?

COLOUR TEST time limit 1 hour

RAINBOW TEST

7 A dark blue circle is worth 3, a yellow circle 4, a pink one 6, a light blue one 5 and a red one 8. Black circles are worth minus 3 each. Follow the arrows from the bottom left circle to the top right circle. Total the circles as you go. What is the lowest you can total?

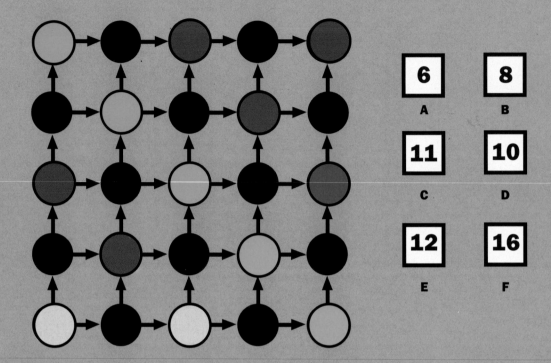

6	8
A	B

11	10
C	D

12	16
E	F

8 Each same box has a value. Work out the logic and discover what should replace the question mark.

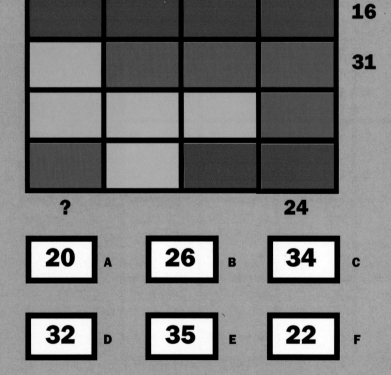

16

31

?   24

20 A	26 B	34 C

32 D	35 E	22 F

RAINBOW TEST

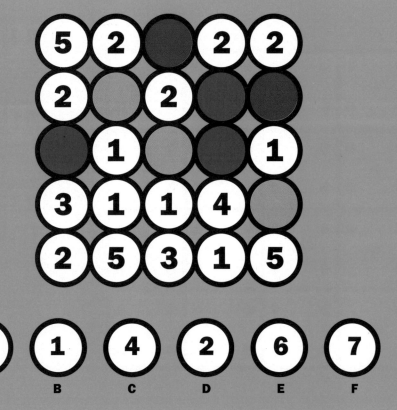

A 3 **B** 1 **C** 4 **D** 2 **E** 6 **F** 7

9 Move from circle to touching circle, starting from the bottom left corner and finishing in the top right corner. A red circle is worth minus 3, a blue one minus 1 and a green one minus 2. Collect nine circles each time and total them. How many different routes are there to total 0?

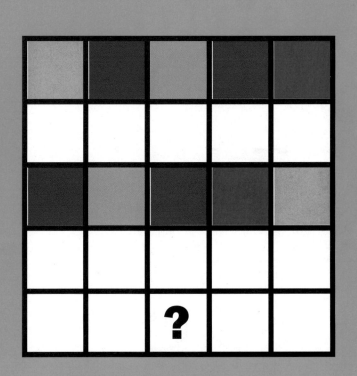

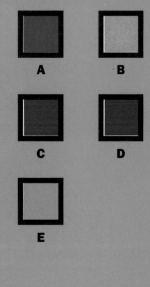

A

B

C

D

E

10 When the square is completed no two identical squares will appear in any row, column or diagonal line. What should replace the question mark?

RAINBOW TEST

11 Which square's contents matches C1?

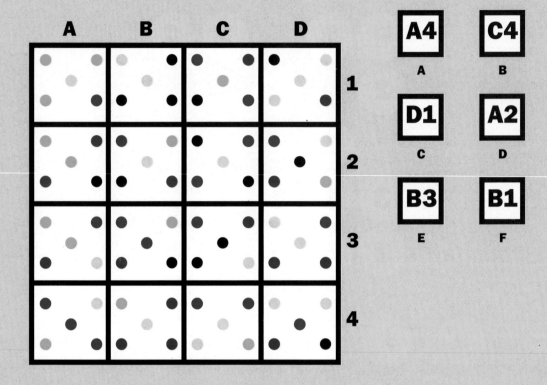

12 Move from oval to touching circle, starting from the bottom left-hand corner finishing in the top right corner. A red circle is worth minus 6, a blue one minus 3, a pink one minus 4, a black one is worth minus 2 and a green one minus 7. Collect nine circles each time and total them. What is the highest number you can possibly total?

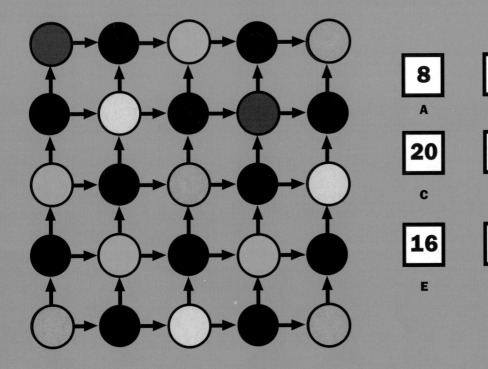

2	3	6	3	1	2
5	3	1	3	1	2
2	1	F	3	1	3
4	1	2	2	1	3
5	1	3	1	2	2
2	1	1	5	3	5
1	6	4	1	1	2

2 A   **3** B

3 C   **1** D

4 E   **1** F

13 Here is an unusual safe. Each of the buttons must be pressed only once in the correct order to open it. The last button is marked F. The number of moves is marked on each button. A pink number means move down. A blue number means move up. A green number means move left and a red number means move right. Thus a blue 1 would mean one move up, while a green 1 would mean one move to the left. Which button is the first you must press?

14 A yellow circle is worth 3, a red circle 4, a green one 5 and an orange one 2. Black circles are worth minus 2 each. Follow the arrows from the bottom left-hand circle to the top right-handcircle. Total the circles as you go. What is the highest you can total?

8 A   **6** B

20 C   **12** D

16 E   **10** F

RAINBOW TEST

15 When the square is completed no two identical squares will appear in any row, column or diagonal line. What should replace the question mark?

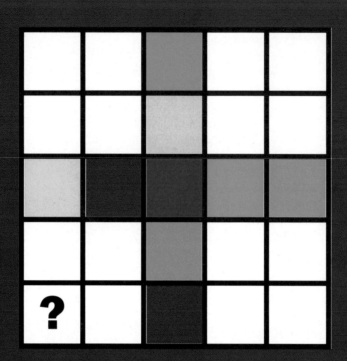

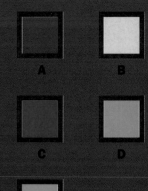

16 Move from circle to touching circle, starting from the bottom left corner and finishing in the top right corner. Collect nine circles each time. How many different routes are there to collect two orange, two pink, two green, two yellow and one black?

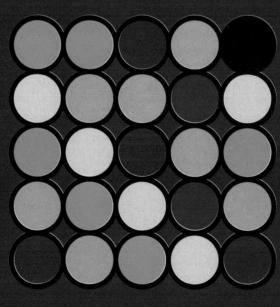

A	B	C	D	E	F
9	6	13	15	12	10

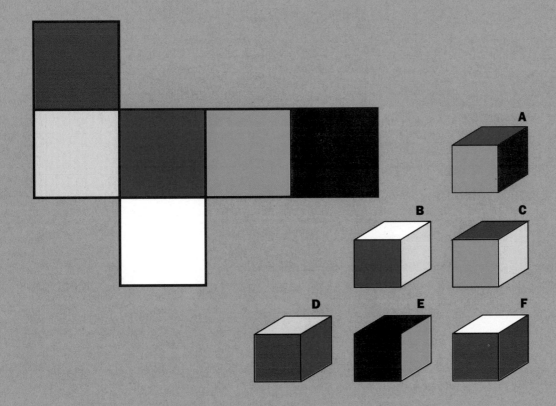

17 Which of the constructed boxes can be made from the pattern?

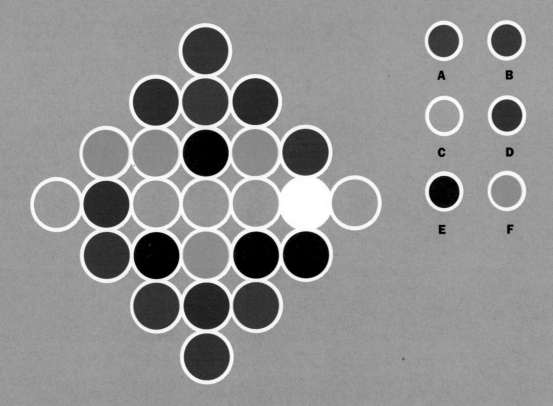

18 Which circle is missing from this series?

RAINBOW TEST

19 Each same box has a value. Work out the logic and discover what should replace the question mark?

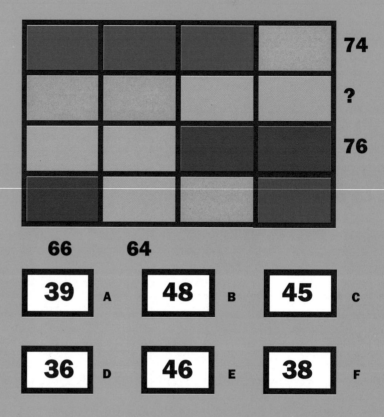

74

?

76

66   64

39 A	48 B	45 C
36 D	46 E	38 F

20 Start at any corner and follow the lines. Collect another four boxes. Green boxes are worth 4 each, pink boxes are worth 2, yellow boxes are worth 3 and dark blue boxes are worth 5. Total the five boxes. What is the highest possible total?

20	15	17	23	19	22
A	B	C	D	E	F

COLOUR TEST time limit 1 hour

RAINBOW TEST

21 Move from circle to touching circle, starting from the bottom left corner and finishing in the top right corner. Collect nine circles each time. How many different routes are there to collect one orange, one red, one blue, three green and three pink?

21	19	16	23	24	28
A	B	C	D	E	F

22 Here is an unusual safe. Each of the buttons must be pressed only once in the correct order to open it. The last button is marked F. The number of moves is marked on each button. A red number means move down. A blue number means move up. A green number means move left and a pink number means move right. Thus a blue 1 would mean one move up, whilst a pink 1 would mean one move to the right. Which button is the first you must press?

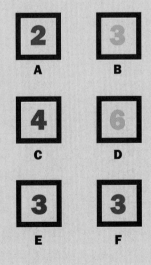

COLOUR TEST time limit 1 hour

RAINBOW TEST

23 Which circle is missing from this series?

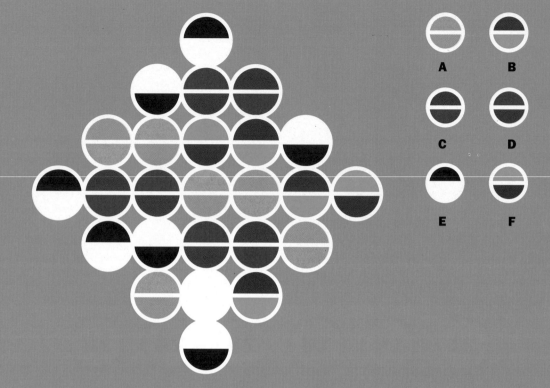

24 Move from circle to touching circle, starting from the bottom left corner and finishing in the top right corner. A yellow circle is worth minus 4, a blue one minus 2, a pink one is worth minus 1 and a green one minus 3. Collect nine circles each time and total them. What is the highest number you can possibly total?

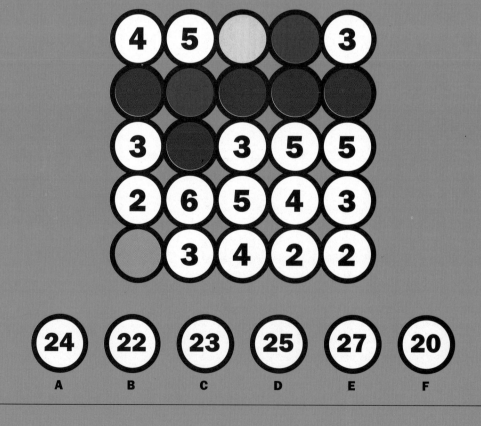

COLOUR TEST time limit 1 hour

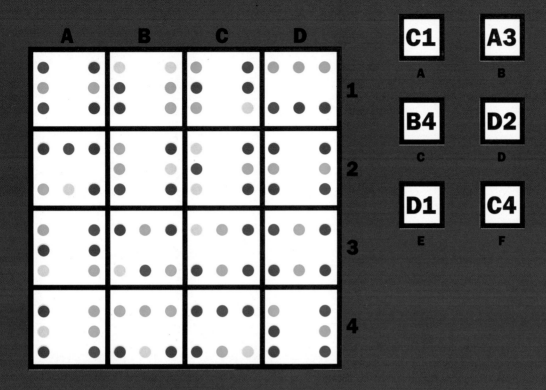

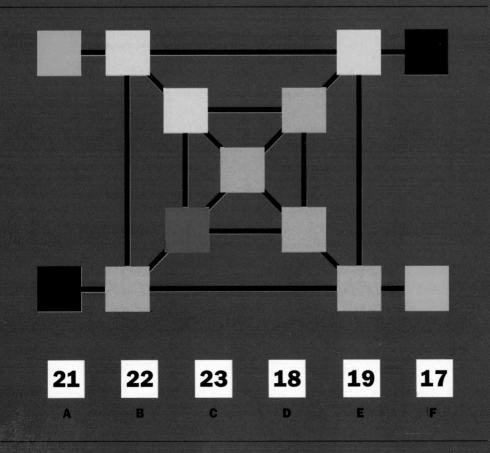

25 Which square's contents matches A2?

26 Start at any corner and follow the lines. Collect another four boxes. Green boxes are worth 3 each, yellow boxes are worth 4, black boxes are worth 2, a blue box is worth 6 and orange boxes are worth 5. Total the five boxes. What is the lowest possible total?

RAINBOW TEST

27 Which of the constructed boxes can be made from the pattern?

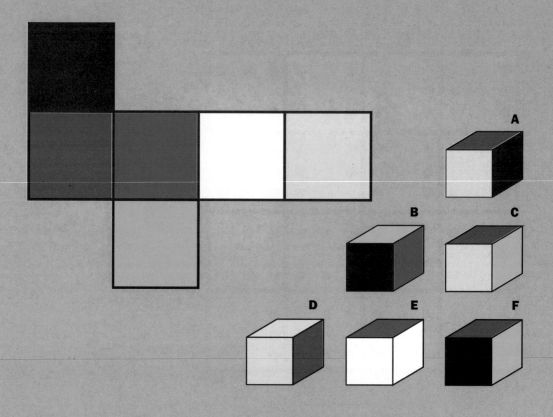

A

B   C

D   E   F

28 Each same box has a value. Work out the logic and discover what should replace the question mark.

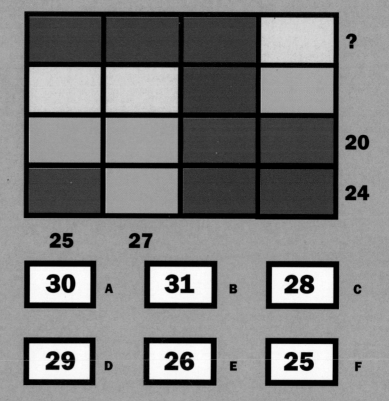

?

20

24

25   27

30 A	31 B	28 C
29 D	26 E	25 F

COLOUR TEST time limit 1 hour

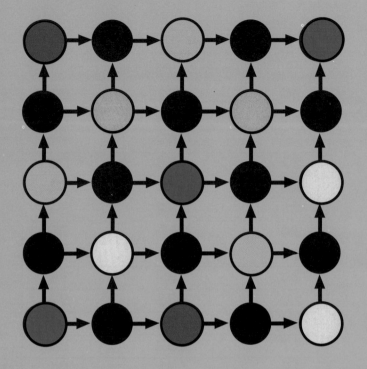

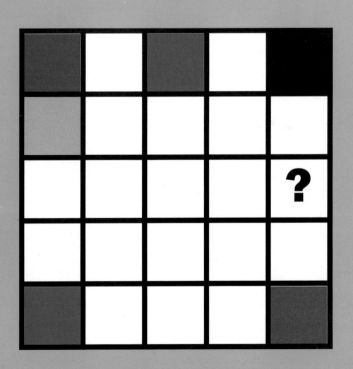

41

A

49

B

45

C

50

D

42

E

53

F

29 A orange circle is worth 7, a red circle 8, a green one 5, a blue circle is worth 6 and a yellow one 4. Black circles are worth 5 each. Follow the arrows from the bottom left circle to the top right circle. Total the circles as you go. What is the lowest you can total?

A

B

C

D

E

30 When the square is completed no two identical squares will appear in any row, column or diagonal line. What should replace the question mark?

RAINBOW TEST ANSWERS

1 B.
2 F. Pink 2 in the third row, third column
3 D. Start at the top, the series reads red, blue, green, black and repeats from left to right.
4 E
5 C.
6 C.
7 D.
8 B. Pink =4, blue =8, green =7.
9 B.
10 A.
11 E.
12 C.
13 F. Pink 1 in the third row, second column.
14 F.
15 D.
16 D.
17 B.
18 A. Start in the extreme left circle. The series, orange, green, pink, red, blue, black, zigzags up and down.
19 E. Blue =23, orange =5, green =18, pink =20.
20 F.
21 A.
22 A. Blue 2 in the fifth row, fourth column.
23 F. Start in the top circle. The series moves across from left to right as follows: Black/white, white/black, blue/red, red/blue, green/orange, orange/green etc.
24 E.
25 F.
26 E.
27 C.
28 D. Green =6, red =4, pink =7, yellow =8.
29 C.
30 B.

SCORE	I.Q.	PERCENTILE
30	161	99
29	160	99
28	157	99
27	155	99
26	154	98
25	152	98
24	150	98
23	148	98*
20	138	95
19	136	94
18	134	93
17	132	92
16	131	91
15	130	90
14	125	85
13	122	80
12	117	75
11	115	70
10	112	65
9	108	60
8	105	55
7	100	50
6	95	45
5	90	40

* MENSA LEVEL
**You should attempt to join
– see front page for details.**

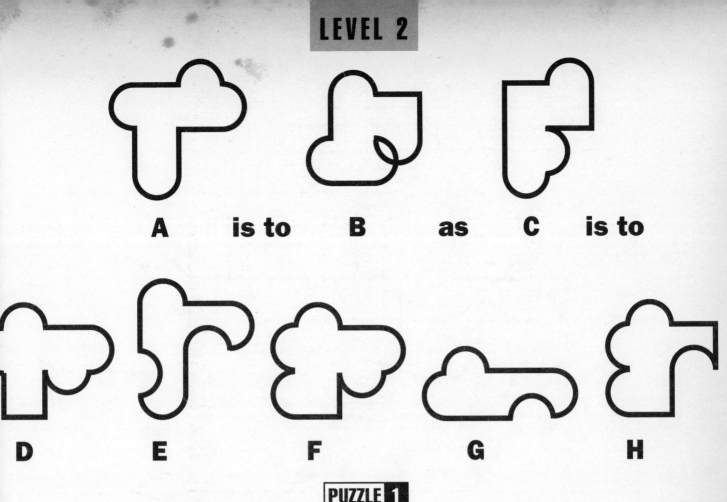

A   is to   B   as   C   is to

D   E   F   G   H

PUZZLE 1

See answer 117

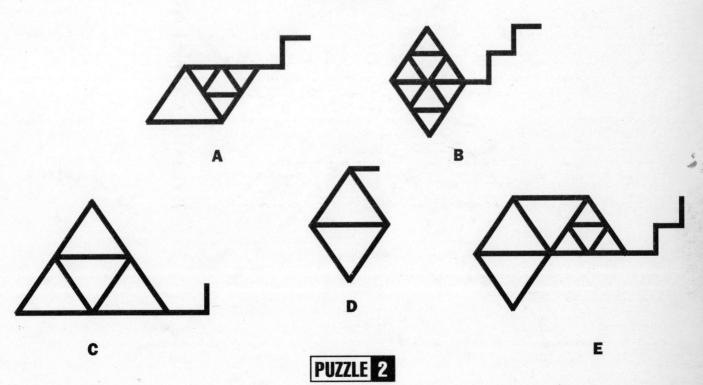

PUZZLE 2

Can you find the odd shape out?

See answer 170

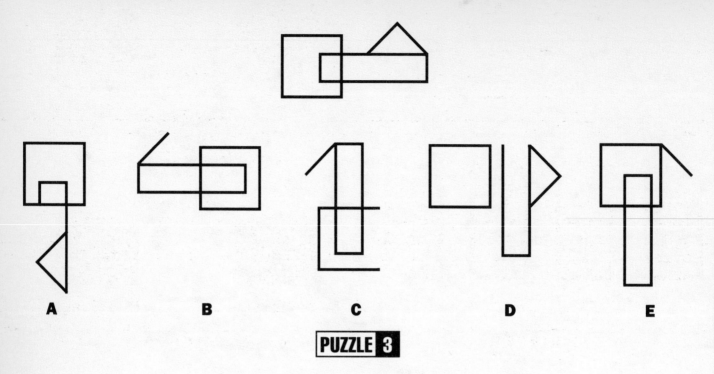

A   B   C   D   E

PUZZLE 3

To which of these diagrams could you add a single straight
line to match the conditions of the above figure?

See answer 145

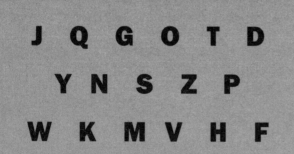

J Q G O T D
Y N S Z P
W K M V H F

PUZZLE 4

Most anagrams give you a heap of mixed up
letters and ask you to sort them out. This one is
different. The letters above are the ones you do
NOT need to complete the puzzle!

See answer 176

PUZZLE 5

The four main mathematical signs have been left out
of this equation. Can you replace them?

See answer 184

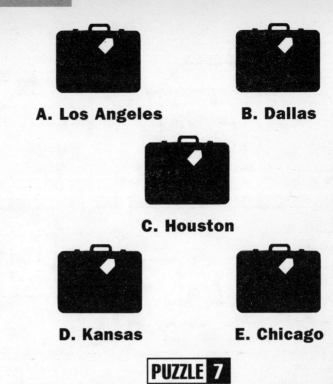

A. Los Angeles   **B. Dallas**

C. Houston

D. Kansas   **E. Chicago**

C	E	G	I
H	J	L	?

PUZZLE 6

Can you unravel the logic behind these domino pieces
and fill in the missing letter?

See answer 122

PUZZLE 7

All the suitcases are shown with their destinations.
Which is the odd one out?

See answer 60

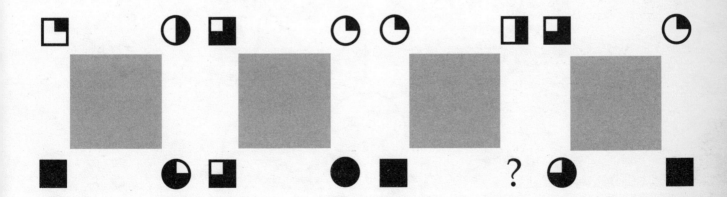

PUZZLE 8

Can you find the shape that should replace the
question mark ?

See answer 9

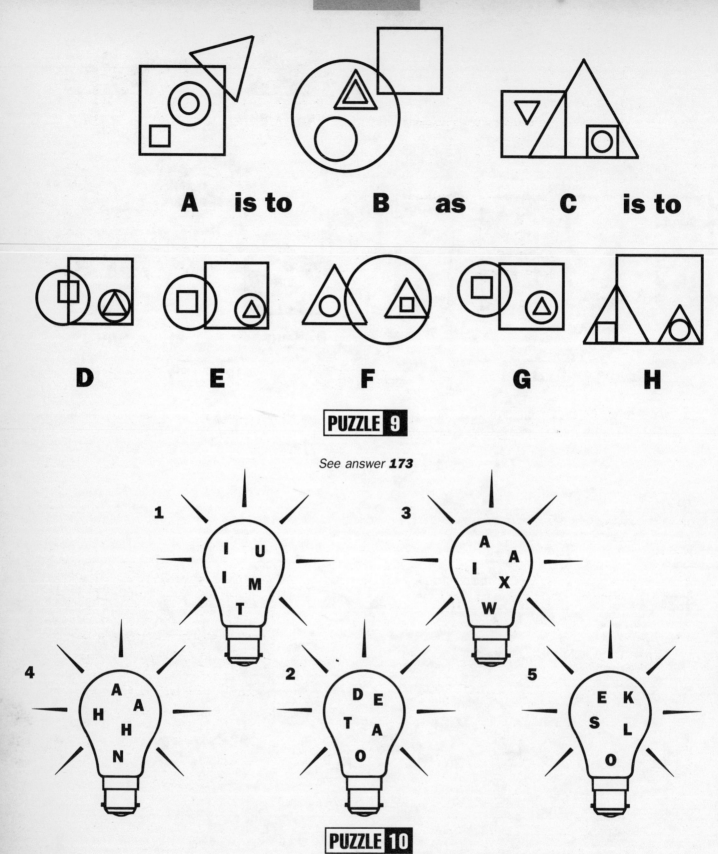

A   is to   B   as   C   is to

D   E   F   G   H

PUZZLE 9

See answer 173

PUZZLE 10

Pick up one letter from each bulb in numerical order. You should find the names of five US states and two dummy letters. What are they?

See answer 46

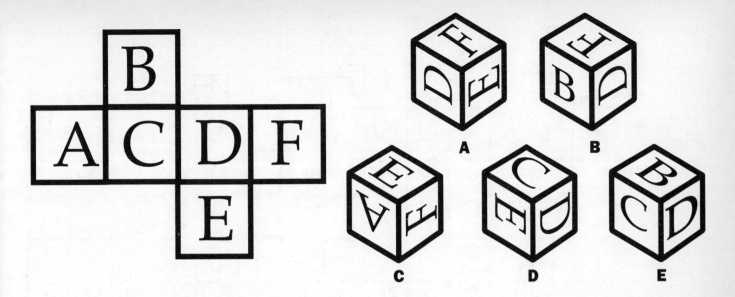

PUZZLE 11

Can you spot the cube that cannot be made
from the layout above?

See answer 167

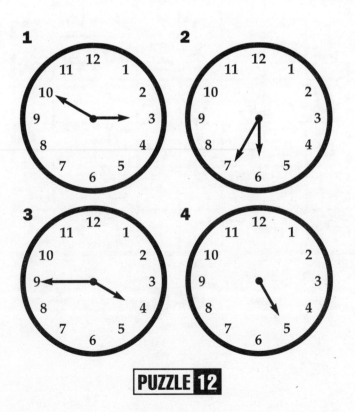

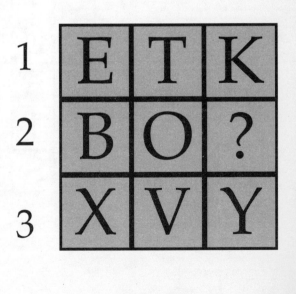

PUZZLE 12

Can you work out which number the missing hand on
clock 4 should point at?

See answer 137

PUZZLE 13

Can you unravel the logic behind this square and
find the missing letter?

See answer 91

Z	R	T	T	U	W	W	Z	Z	S	Z	R	T	T	U	W
S	Z	Z	W	W	U	T	T	R	Z	S	Z	Z	W	W	U
Z	S	Z	R	T	T	U	W	W	Z	Z	S	Z	R	T	T
Z	W	W	U	T	T	R	Z	S	Z	Z	W	W	U	T	T
W	Z	Z	S	Z	R	T	T			Z	Z	S	Z	R	
W	U	T	T	R	Z	S	Z			U	T	T	R	Z	
U	W	W	Z	Z	S	Z	R			W	W	Z	Z	S	
T	T	R	Z	S	Z	Z	W	W	U	T	T	R	Z	S	Z
T	T	U	W	W	Z	Z	S	Z	R	T	T	U	W	W	Z
R	Z	S	Z	Z	W	W	U	T	T	R	Z	S	Z	Z	W
Z	R	T	T	U	W	W	Z	Z	S	Z	R	T	T	U	W
S	Z	Z	W	W	U	T	T	R	Z	S	Z	Z	W	W	U
Z	S	Z	R	T	T	U	W	W	Z	Z	S	Z	R	T	T
Z	W	W	U	T	T	R	Z	S	Z	Z	W	W	U	T	T
W	Z	Z	S	Z	R	T	T	U	W	W	Z	Z	S	Z	R
W	U	T	T	R	Z	S	Z	Z	W	W	U	T	T	R	Z

PUZZLE 14

Can you spot the pattern of this grid and complete the missing section?

See answer 115

102

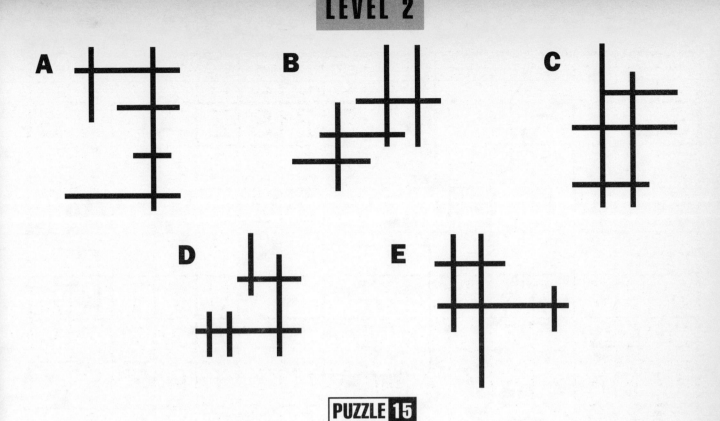

A **B** **C**

D **E**

PUZZLE 15

Can you work out which diagram is the odd one out?

See answer 179

A. 4 hrs 20 min

B. 3 hrs 15 min

C. 6 hrs 14 min

?

80

60

D. 7 hrs 13 min

E. 4 hrs 12 min

42

78

PUZZLE 16

Each tractor has been working for the time shown.
The figure under the tractor shows how many tons
of potatoes have been gathered. Clearly some
strange logic is at work! How many tons has
tractor A gathered?

See answer 90

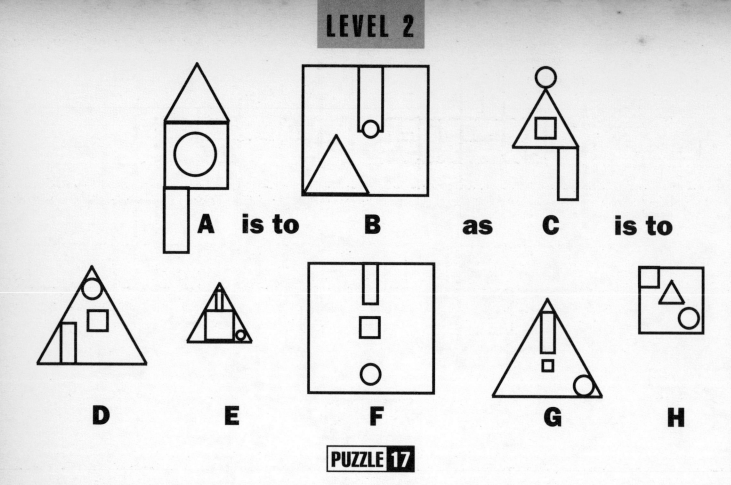

A is to B as C is to

D   E   F   G   H

PUZZLE 17

See answer 106

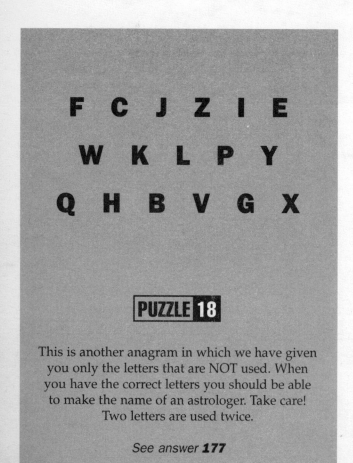

F C J Z I E

W K L P Y

Q H B V G X

PUZZLE 18

This is another anagram in which we have given you only the letters that are NOT used. When you have the correct letters you should be able to make the name of an astrologer. Take care! Two letters are used twice.

See answer 177

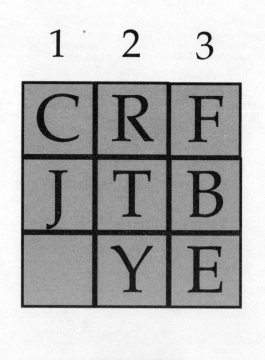

1   2   3

C	R	F
J	T	B
	Y	E

PUZZLE 19

Can you work out the logic behind this square and complete the missing section?

See answer 93

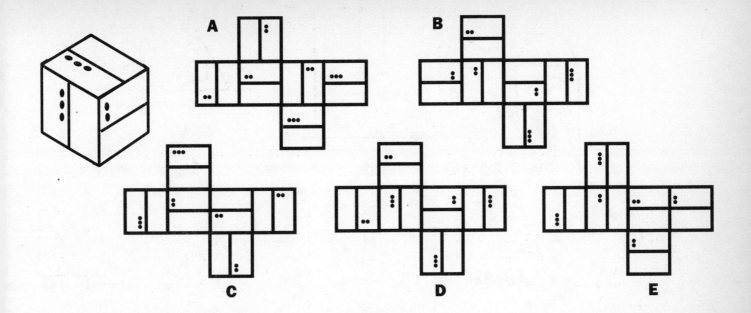

PUZZLE 20

Which of these layouts could be used to make the above cube?

See answer 149

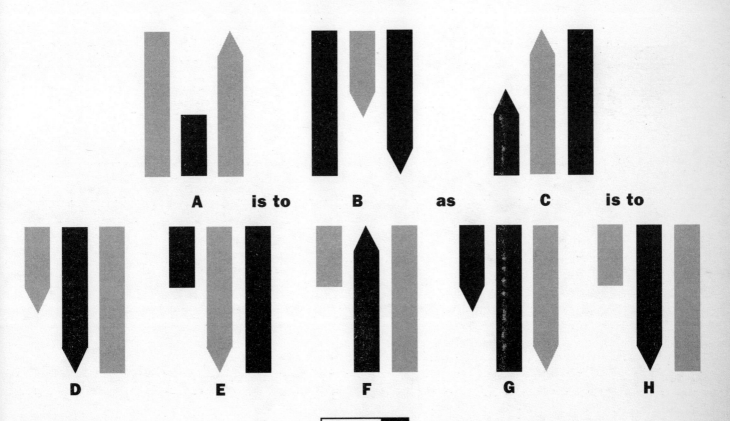

A   is to   B   as   C   is to

PUZZLE 21

See answer 178

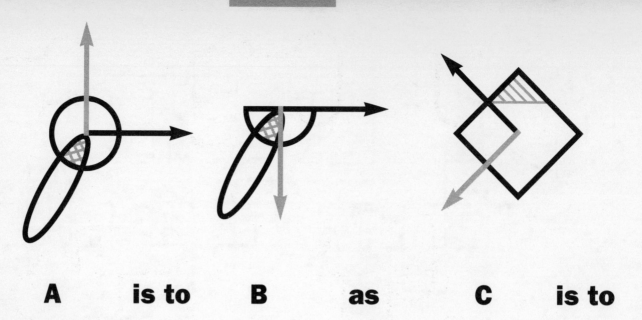

A   is to   B   as   C   is to

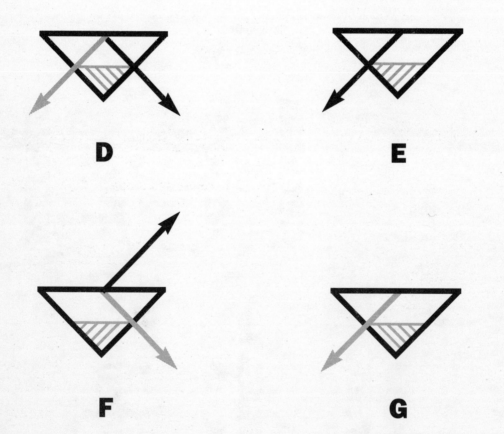

D

E

F

G

A

B

C

D

E

PUZZLE 23

Can you find the odd shape out?

See answer 185

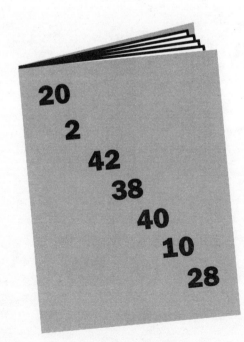

20
2
42
38
40
10
28

PUZZLE 24

No. 139
Silverstone

No. 101
Monaco

No. 98
Le Mans

No. 154
Monte Carlo

No. ?
Indianapolis

PUZZLE 25

Can you unravel the code on this book to find its famous author?

See answer 131

These cars are all racing at famous circuits. Can you work out the number of the car at Indianapolis?

See answer 85

A   is to   **B**   as   **C**   is to

D

E

F

G

H

PUZZLE 26

See answer 154

MOUSSAKA	RISOTTO	TIRAMISU
A	B	C

LASAGNE	CHOW MEIN
D	E

COQ AU VIN	VINDALOO
F	G

PUZZLE 27

Can you work out which of the above dishes is
the odd one out?

See answer 35

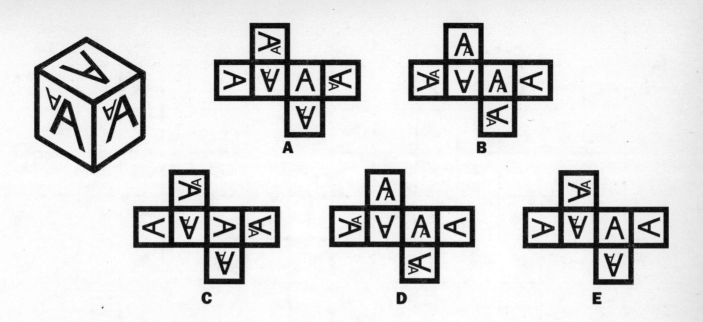

PUZZLE 28

Which of the following layouts could be used to make the above cube?

See answer 181

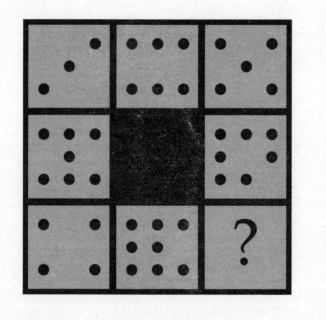

PUZZLE 29

Can you work out the logic behind this square and fill in the missing section?

See answer 92

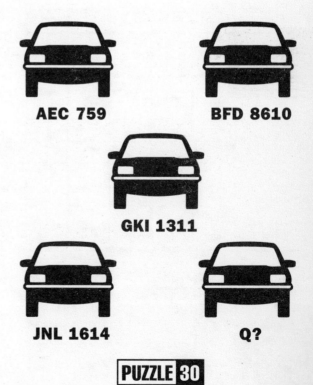

AEC 759

BFD 8610

GKI 1311

JNL 1614

Q?

PUZZLE 30

The registration plates of all these cars conform to a certain logic. Can you work out the final plate?

See answer 84

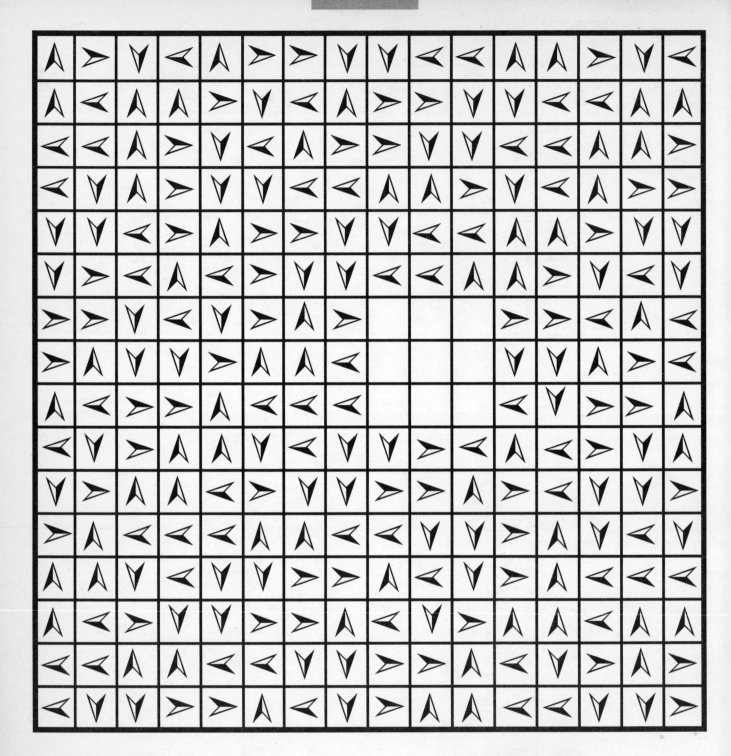

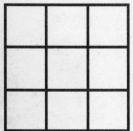

PUZZLE 31

Can you work out the reasoning behind this grid and complete the missing section?

See answer 182

A

B

C

D

E

PUZZLE 32

Can you work out which is the odd diagram out?

See answer 153

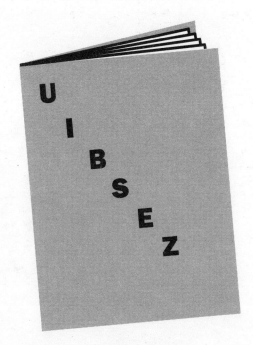

U
I
B
S
E
Z

PUZZLE 33

Can you work out the reasoning behind this code and discover the author of this book?

See answer 123

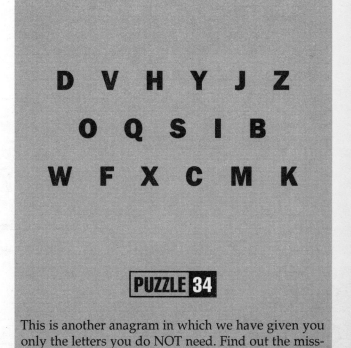

D V H Y J Z

O Q S I B

W F X C M K

PUZZLE 34

This is another anagram in which we have given you only the letters you do NOT need. Find out the missing letters, change their order, and you will have the name of a giant. One letter is used twice. Extra clue: his father also appears in this book.

See answer 171

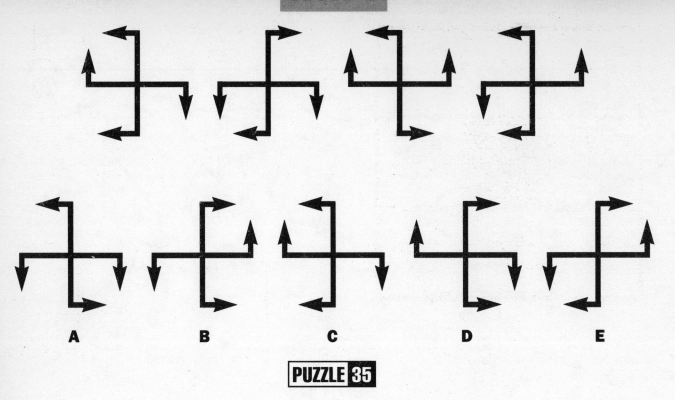

A   B   C   D   E

PUZZLE 35

Can you work out which of these symbols comes next in
this sequence?

See answer 104

Politiken

La Stampa

El Pais

Il Giorno

The Independent

PUZZLE 36

Each balloon has been sponsored by a famous newspaper.
The number is somehow linked to the paper's name. What
is the number of *The Independent's* balloon?

See answer 78

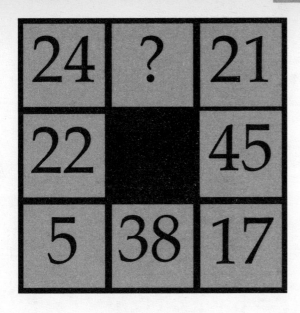

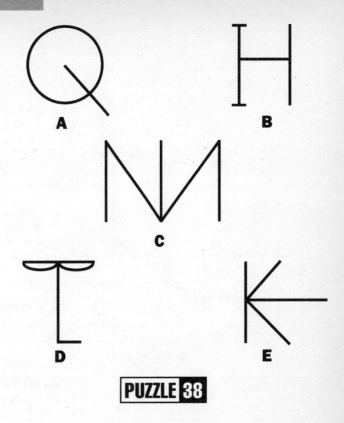

PUZZLE 37

Can you work out the logic behind this square and find the missing number?

See answer 80

PUZZLE 38

Can you work out which symbol is the odd one out?

See answer 155

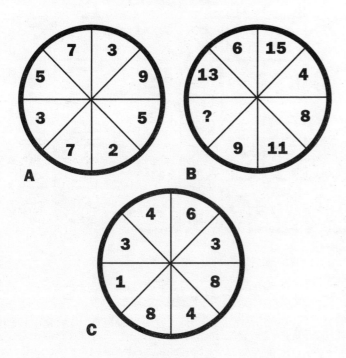

PUZZLE 39

Can you replace the question mark with a number?

See answer 111

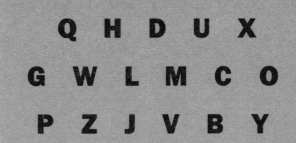

Q H D U X

G W L M C O

P Z J V B Y

PUZZLE 40

This is another anagram in which we haven given you only the letters you do NOT need. Find the missing letters, rearrange them, and you should find the name of the hero of a Gothic novel. The N is used more than once and one other letter is repeated.

See answer 172

LEVEL 2

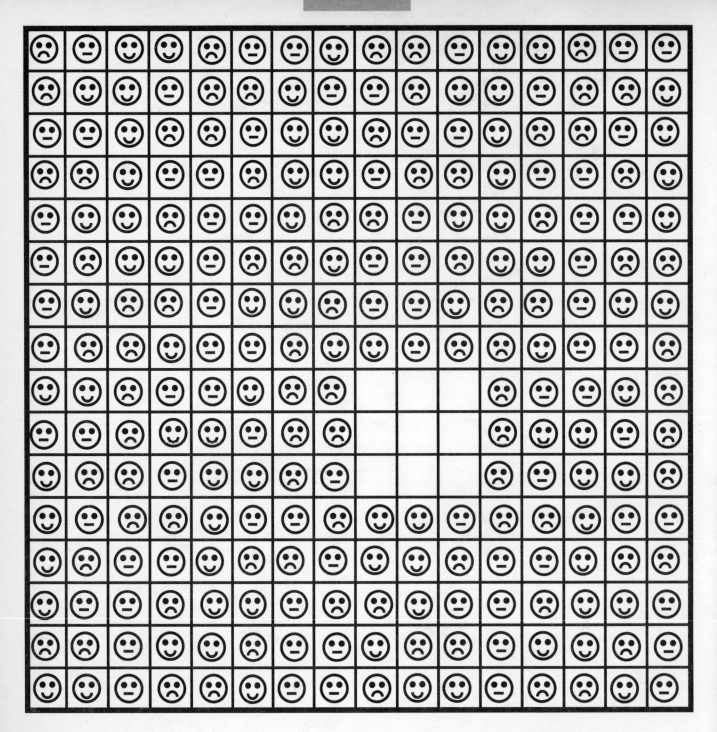

PUZZLE 41

This grid is made up according to a certain pattern. Can you work it out and fill in the missing section?

See answer 42

114

M NN B

A is to B as C is to

CC CC B A BB

D E F G H

PUZZLE 42

See answer 180

PUZZLE 43

Can you work out what the next matchstick man in this series should look like?

See answer 53

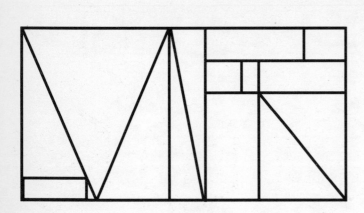

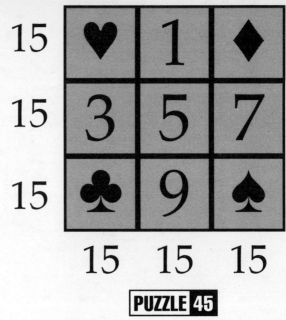

PUZZLE 44

Can you work out how many rectangles can be found in this diagram altogether?

See answer 56

PUZZLE 45

Can you work out how much each shape is worth?

See answer 45

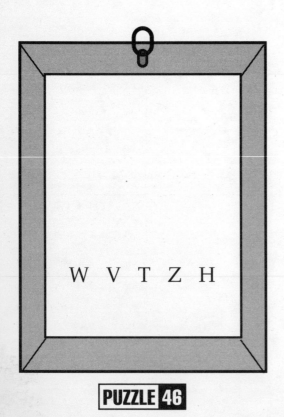

W V T Z H

PUZZLE 46

Can you unravel the code on the back of the picture to find the name of its artist.

See answer 102

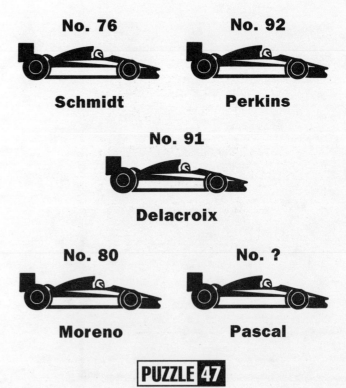

PUZZLE 47

Each car's number is related to its driver's name. Can you predict which car Pascal will drive?

See answer 79

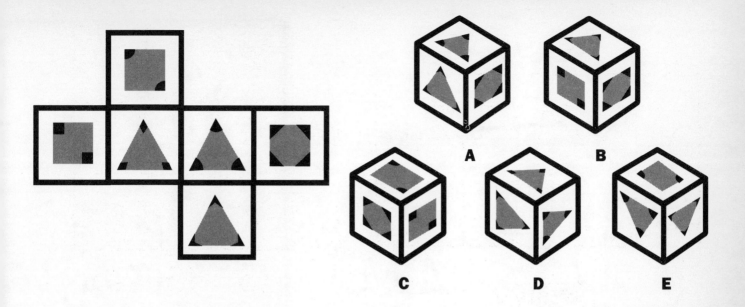

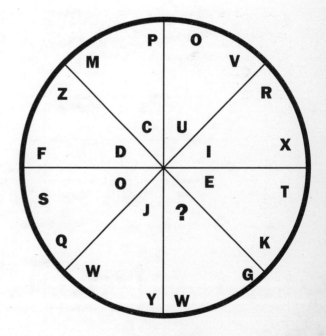

PUZZLE 48

Can you work out which of these cubes cannot be made from the above layout?

See answer 165

RDPNHVEE
FLBFILOAU
AWADNSAGI
ELTSBNOO
PSTAEELTH
IMAMAII

PUZZLE 49

The above are all anagrams of American towns. However, two extra letters have been added to each word. If you collect all the extra letters you will be able to make another place name.

See answer 18

PUZZLE 50

Can you replace the question mark with a letter?

See answer 183

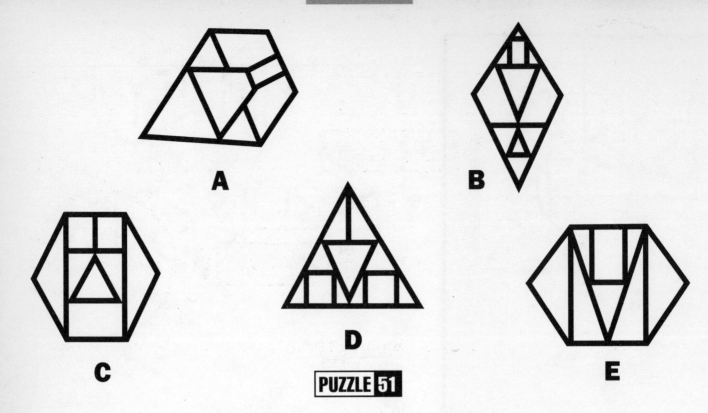

A

B

C

D

E

PUZZLE 51

Can you work out which shape is the odd one out?

See answer **169**

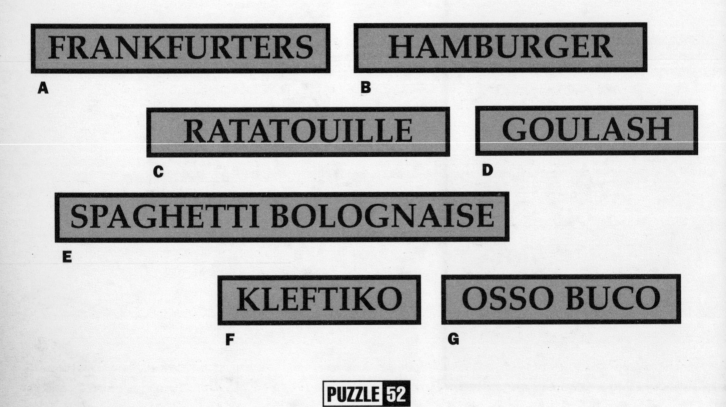

FRANKFURTERS

A

HAMBURGER

B

RATATOUILLE

C

GOULASH

D

SPAGHETTI BOLOGNAISE

E

KLEFTIKO

F

OSSO BUCO

G

PUZZLE 52

Can you work out which of these dishes is the odd one out?

See answer **21**

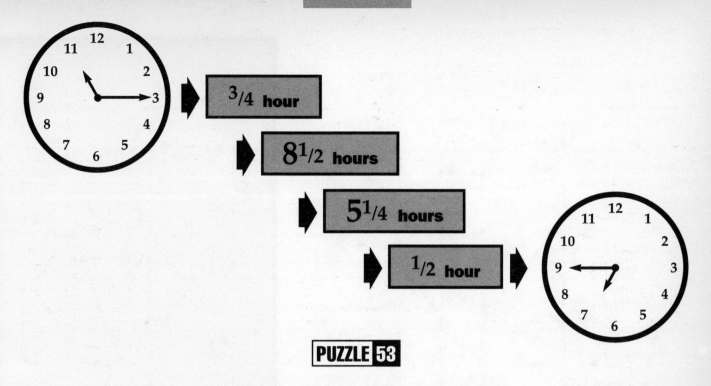

PUZZLE 53

Can you work out, using the amounts of time specified,
whether you have to go forward or backward to get from
the top clock to the bottom clock?

See answer 187

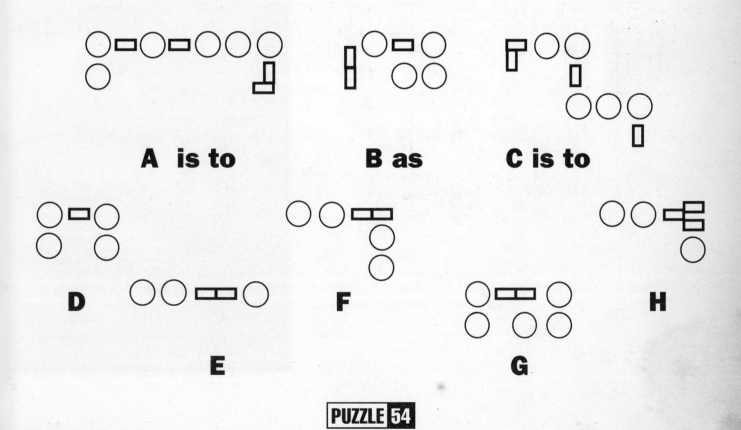

A is to   **B as**   **C is to**

D   **F**   **H**

E   **G**

PUZZLE 54

See answer 186

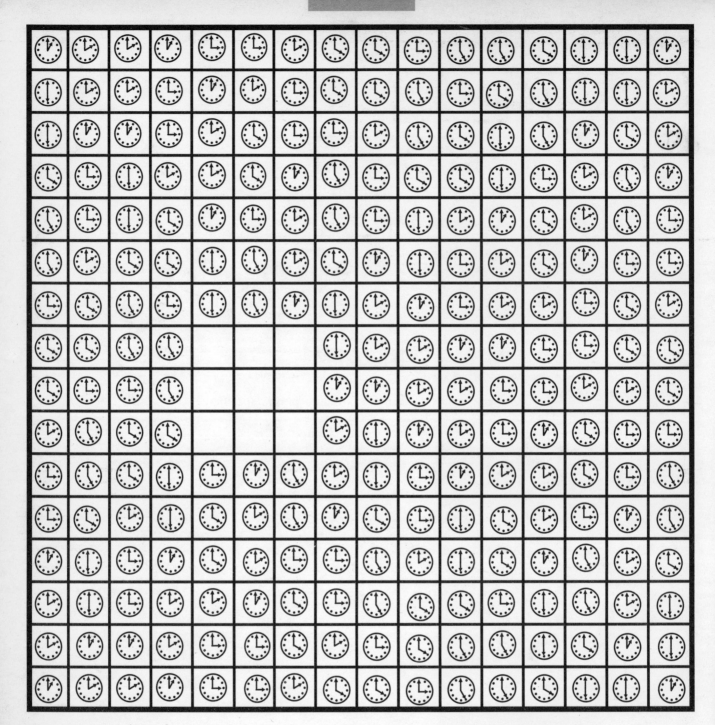

PUZZLE 55

Can you work out which pattern this grid follows and complete the missing section?

See answer **164**

PUZZLE 56

Pick one letter from each cloud in order. You should be able to make the names of five composers.

See answer 41

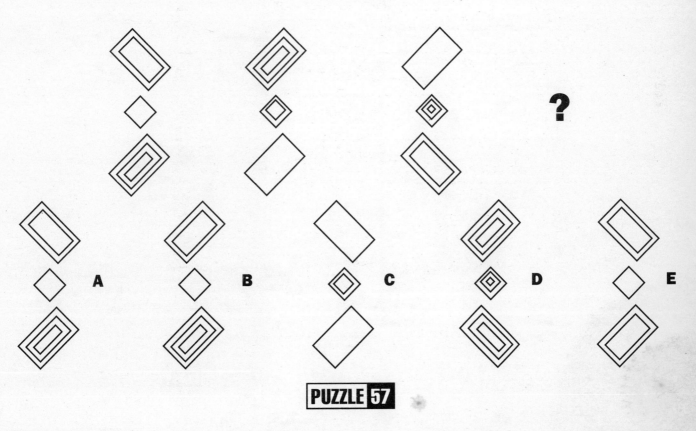

PUZZLE 57

Can you find the column that comes next in the sequence?

See answer 175

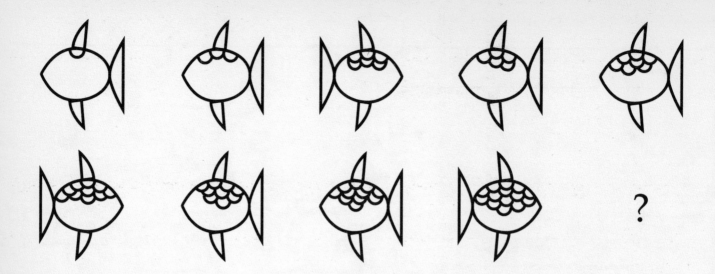

PUZZLE 58

Can you work out what the next fish in this sequence
should look like?

See answer 52

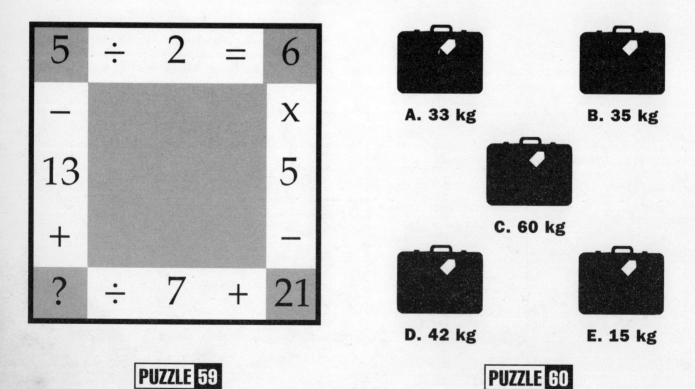

A. 33 kg

B. 35 kg

C. 60 kg

D. 42 kg

E. 15 kg

PUZZLE 59

Can you work out which number should replace the
question mark?

See answer 144

PUZZLE 60

The weight of each suitcase is shown. Which is the
odd one out?

See answer 67

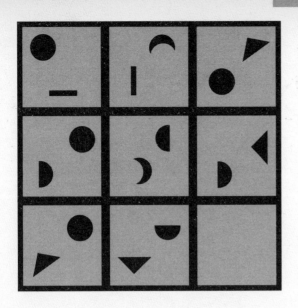

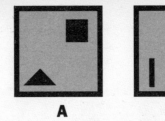

PUZZLE 61

Can you work out which of these squares would complete
the above diagram?

See answer **160**

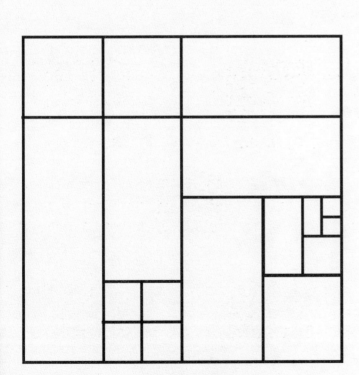

PUZZLE 62

How many squares can you find in this diagram
altogether?

See answer **97**

PUZZLE 63

In this diagram the four basic mathematical
signs (+, −, x, ÷) have been missed out.
Can you replace the question marks?

See answer **136**

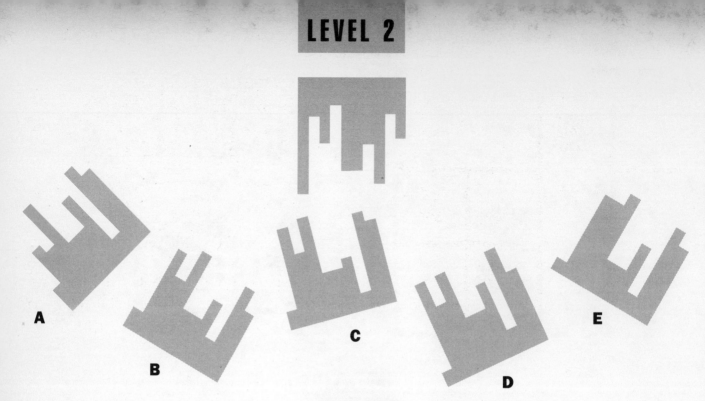

PUZZLE 64

Can you work out which of these shapes would fit together
with the shape above?

See answer 116

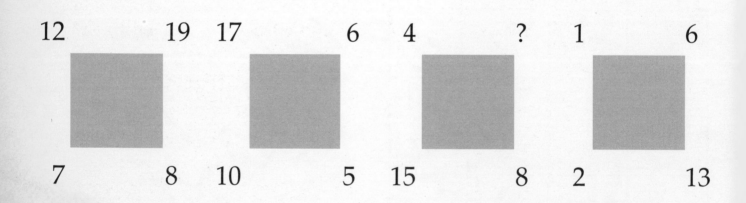

12   19 17   6   4   ?   1   6

7   8 10   5   15   8   2   13

PUZZLE 65

Can you work out the reasoning behind these squares and
replace the question mark with a number?

See answer 120

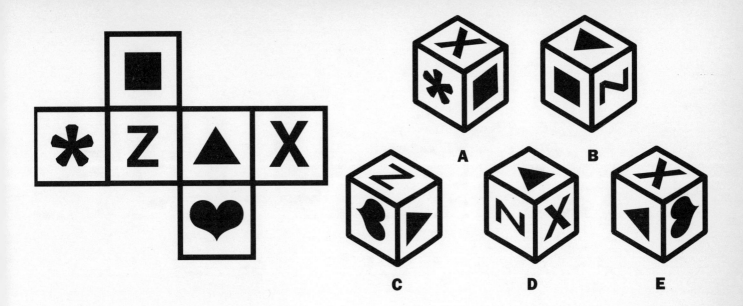

Can you spot the cube that cannot be made from the above layout?

See answer 163

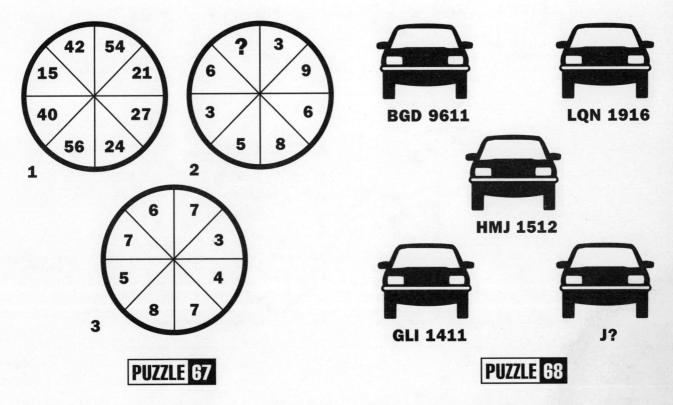

PUZZLE 67

PUZZLE 68

Can you find the number that should replace the question mark?

See answer 121

There is a logic to the registration plates of these cars. What is the plate on the last car?

See answer 77

5	6	9
4	3	2
0	7	1

8	4	12
2	6	0
0	10	4

4	9	6
22	7	11
2	14	1

A   **is to**   **B**   **as**   **C**   **is to**

8	18	12
44	14	22
4	28	2

D

7	7	9
25	5	9
5	17	0

E

7	12	9
25	10	14
5	17	4

F

2	12	4
20	10	14
0	12	4

G

PUZZLE 69

*See answer **88***

126

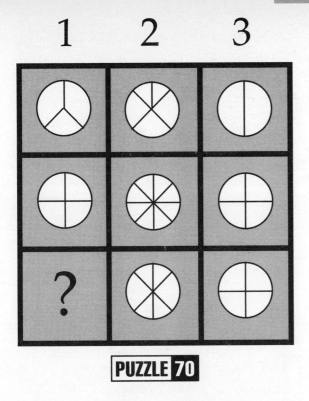

1 2 3

PUZZLE 70

Can you work out the reasoning behind this square and replace the question mark with the correct shape?

See answer **36**

A E

F H

I K

L ?

PUZZLE 71

Can you find the letter that comes next in this series?

See answer **64**

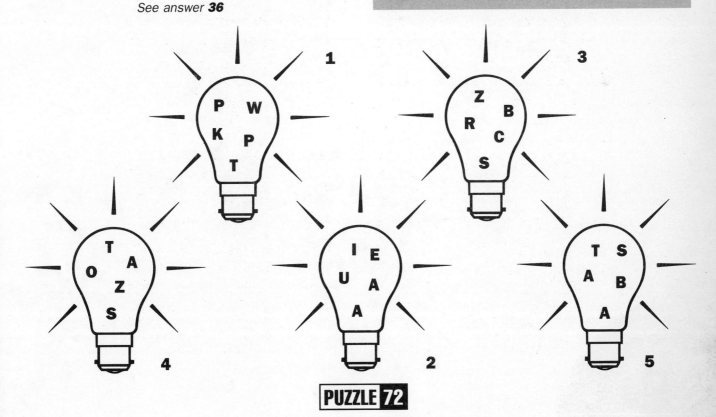

PUZZLE 72

Take one letter from each bulb in order. You should be able to make five five-letter words related to food.

See answer **40**

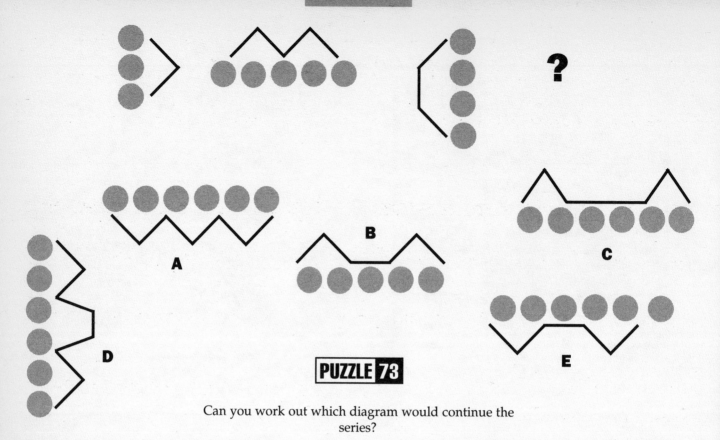

PUZZLE 73

Can you work out which diagram would continue the series?

See answer 161

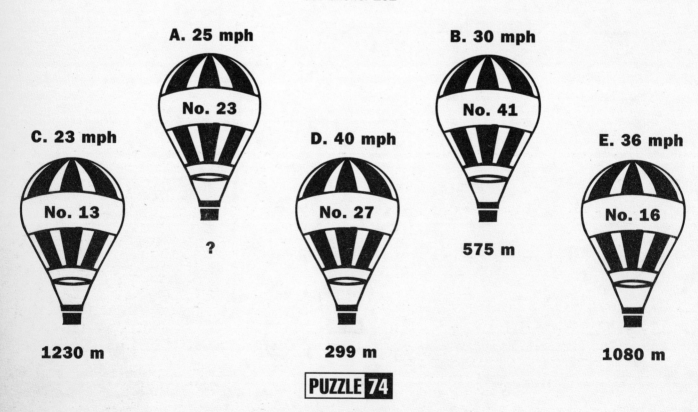

PUZZLE 74

The diagram gives the speed, number and distance covered for each balloon. Can you work out the distance for A?

See answer 69

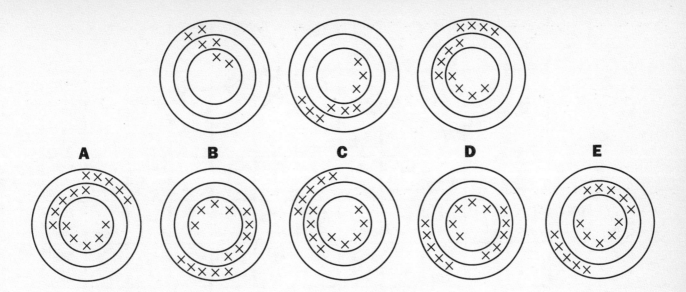

A   B   C   D   E

PUZZLE 75

Can you work out which of these symbols
follows the sequence?

See answer 105

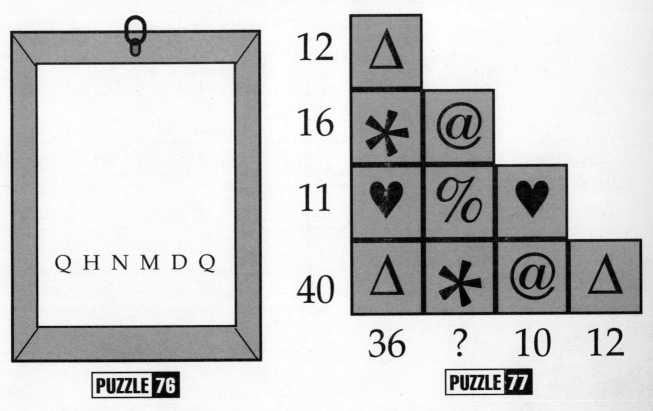

Q H N M D Q

PUZZLE 76

Can you unravel this code and find the
painter of this picture?

See answer 96

PUZZLE 77

Can you work out which number should replace the
question mark in this diagram?

See answer 26

2	2	3	1	1	7	1	4	5	5	2	2	3	1	1	7
5	3	1	1	7	1	4	5	5	2	2	3	1	1	7	1
5	2	3	1	1	7	1	4	5	5	2	2	3	1	1	4
4	2	2	2	2	3	1	1	7	1	4	5	5	2	7	5
1	5	2	5	1	4	5	5	2	2	3	1	1	2	1	5
7	5	5	5	7	2	2	3	1	1	7	1	7	3	4	2
1	4	5	4	1	5	3	1	1	7	1	4	1	1	5	2
1	1	4	1	1	5	2	3	1	1	4	5	4	1	5	3
3	7	1	7	3	4	2	2	2	7	5	5	5	7	2	1
2	1	7	1	2	1	5	5	4	1	5	2	5	1	2	1
2	1	1	1	2	7	1	1	3	2	2	2	2	4	3	7
5	3	1	3	5	5	4	1	7	1	1	3	2	5	1	1
5	2	3	2	2	5	5	4	1	7	1	1	3	5	1	4
			2	5	5	4	1	7	1	1	3	2	2	7	5
			4	1	7	1	1	3	2	2	5	5	4	1	5
			3	2	2	5	5	4	1	7	1	1	3	2	2

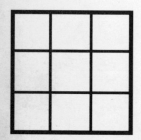

PUZZLE 78

Can you work out the reasoning behind this grid and complete the missing section?

See answer 135

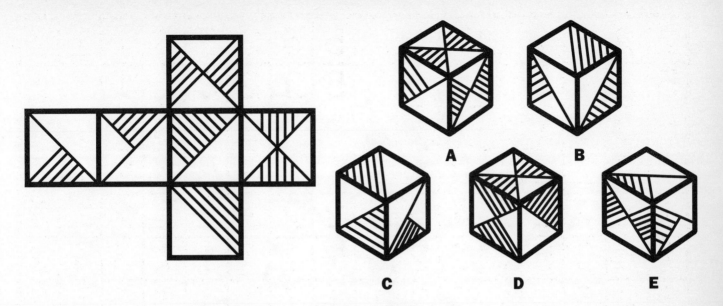

PUZZLE 79

Which of these cubes can be made from the
above layout?

See answer 128

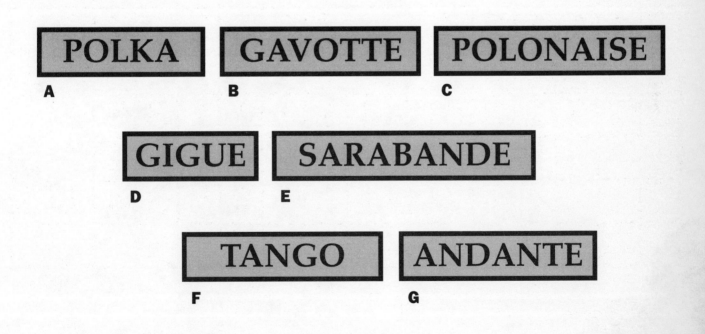

PUZZLE 80

Can you work out which of these musical terms
is the odd one out?

See answer 20

PUZZLE 81

Take one letter from each cloud in order.
You should be able to find five words from around
the world that are in common use.

See answer 50

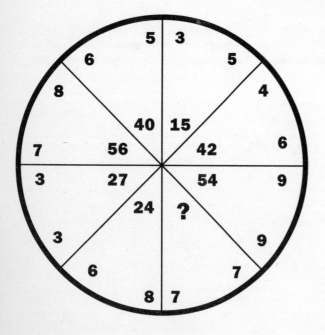

PUZZLE 82

Can you work out the reasoning behind this wheel
and replace the question mark with a number?

See answer 151

Earl left Dallas for a holiday in the UK. He liked Cambridge but not Oxford. He visited Derby but not Nottingham. He went to St Ives but not Polzeath.

Did he like Swansea?

PUZZLE 83

See answer 159

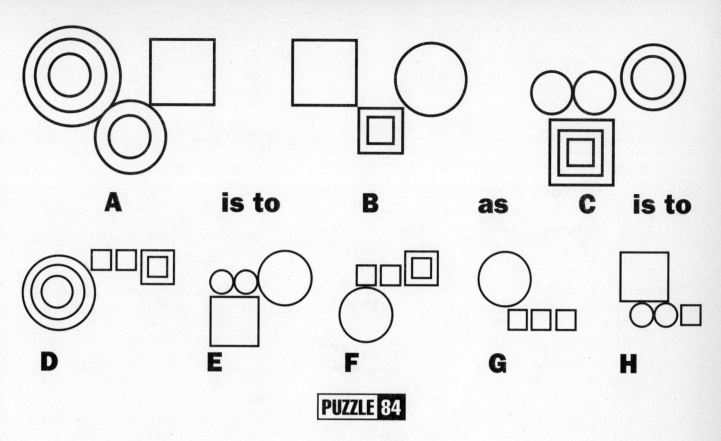

A   is to   **B**   as   **C**   is to

D   **E**   **F**   **G**   **H**

PUZZLE 84

See answer 156

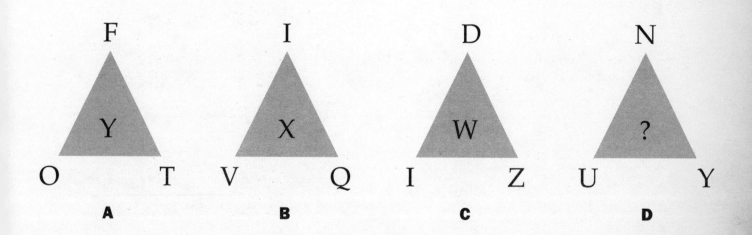

A   **B**   **C**   **D**

PUZZLE 85

Can you work out which letter should replace
the question mark?

See answer 119

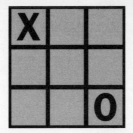 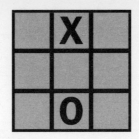

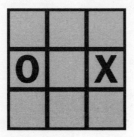 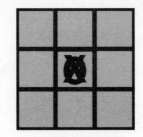 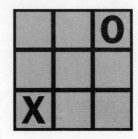

PUZZLE 86

Can you work out what the next grid in this
sequence should look like?

See answer 54

PUZZLE 87

Can you work out what the missing section
in the last wheel should look like?

See answer 57

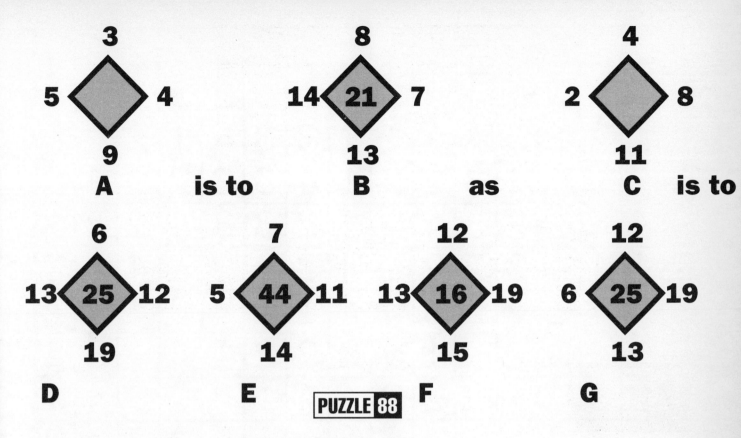

3

5 4

9

A is to

8

14 **21** 7

13

B as

4

2 8

11

C is to

6

13 **25** 12

19

D

7

5 **44** 11

14

E

12

13 **16** 19

15

F

12

6 **25** 19

13

G

PUZZLE 88

See answer 94

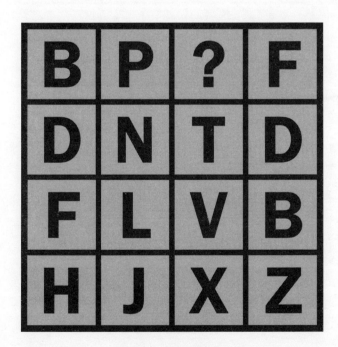

PUZZLE 89

Can you find the letter which completes
this diagram?

See answer 75

No. 4 15kg

No. 7 18kg

No. 3 14kg

No. 8 19kg

No. ? 24kg

PUZZLE 90

Each horse carries a weight handicap.
Can you work out the number of the final horse?

See answer 15

1	2	2	3	4	4	1	2	3	3	4	1	2	2	3	4
3	3	2	1	4	4	3	2	2	1	4	3	3	2	1	4
4	1	2	2	3	4	4	1	2	3	3	4	1	2	2	3
3	2	1	4	4	3	2	2	1	4	3	3	2	1	4	4
3	4	1	2	2	3	4	4	1	2	3	3	4	1	2	2
2	1	4	4	3	2	2	1	4	3	3	2	1	4	4	3
3	3	4	1	2	2	3	4	4	1	2	3	3	4	1	2
1	4	4	3	2	2	1	4	3	3	2	1	4	4	3	2
2	3	3	4	1	2	2	3	4	4	1	2	3	3	4	1
4	4	3	2	2	1	4				1	4	4	3	2	2
1	2	3	3	4	1	2				4	1	2	3	3	4
4	3	2	2	1	4	3				4	4	3	2	2	1
4	1	2	3	3	4	1	2	2	3	4	4	1	2	3	3
3	2	2	1	4	3	3	2	1	4	4	3	2	2	1	4
4	4	1	2	3	3	4	1	2	2	3	4	4	1	2	3
2	2	1	4	3	3	2	1	4	4	3	2	2	1	4	3

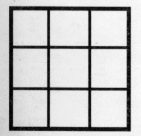

PUZZLE 91

Can you work out the reasoning behind this grid
and complete the missing section?

See answer **51**

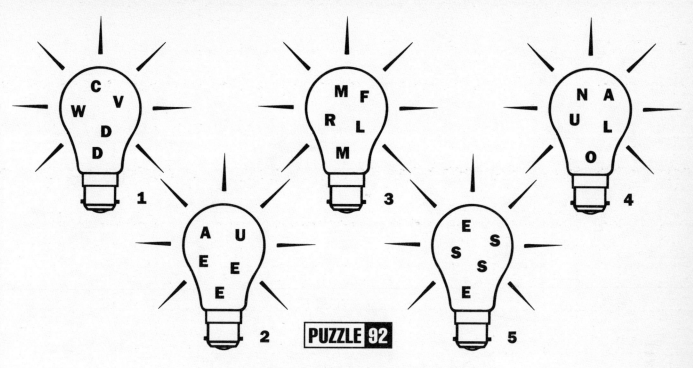

PUZZLE 92

Pick a letter from each bulb in turn and make
the names of five novelists.

*See answer **30***

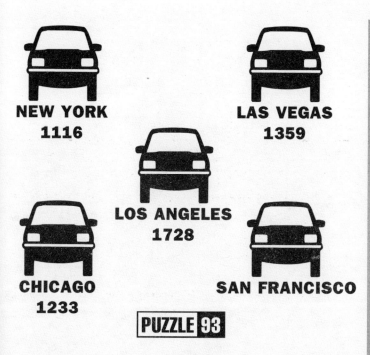

NEW YORK
1116

LAS VEGAS
1359

LOS ANGELES
1728

CHICAGO
1233

SAN FRANCISCO

PUZZLE 93

All these cars started from the same place and drove to
the cities indicated. The mileages shown on the trip
meter seem to make no sense, but the logic comes from
the names of the destinations. Can you work out what
it is, and the mileage of the last car?

*See answer **68***

1. M R V N O A E C
2. D O N I G F E I L
3. T V T A L N N A R A A I
4. O O E N H L I N G R A
5. G D I I I V O B O S U N R O

PUZZLE 94

Here are five anagrams of well-known operas.
However, two additional letters are hidden in
each one, which when put together, make up
a new opera. To help you, the first letter of the
new opera is a D (not included in any of the
anagrams).

*See answer **7***

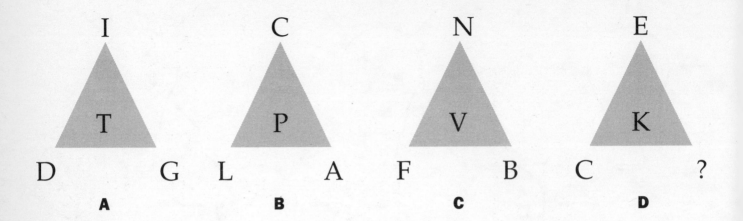

PUZZLE 95

Can you find the letter that should replace
the question mark?

See answer 109

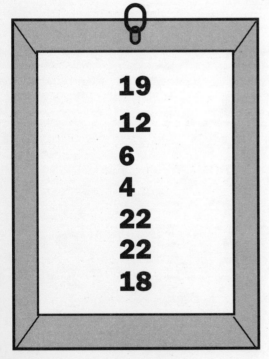

19
12
6
4
22
22
18

PUZZLE 96

Can you work out the reasoning behind this code
and find the artist of this painting?

See answer 87

Sam took a holiday in the United States. He liked Idaho but hated Texas. He enjoyed Hawaii but not Arkansas. He loved California but not Wisconsin.

Did he like Illinois?

PUZZLE 97

See answer 158

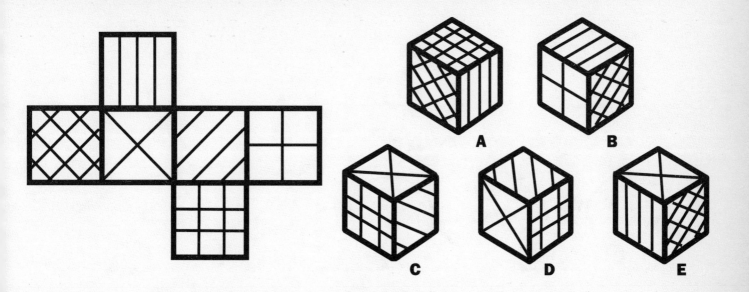

PUZZLE 98

Can you work out which of these cubes cannot be
made from the this layout?

See answer 118

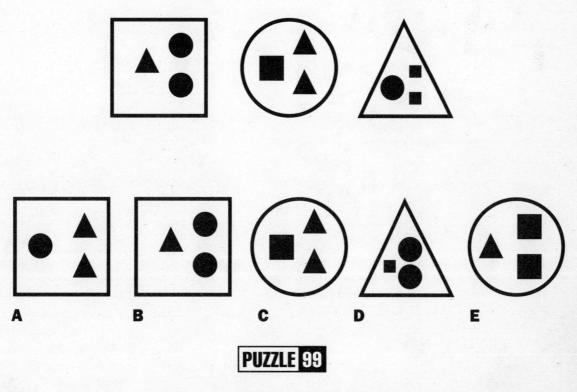

PUZZLE 99

Can you find the shape that would continue the series above?

See answer 150

PUZZLE 100

Take one letter from each cloud in order.
You should be able to make the names of five scientists.

See answer 58

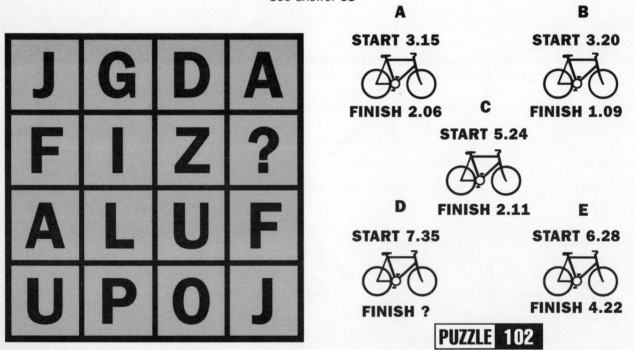

J	G	D	A
F	I	Z	?
A	L	U	F
U	P	O	J

PUZZLE 101

Can you work out which letter should replace the
question mark in this square?

See answer 62

A
START 3.15
FINISH 2.06

B
START 3.20
FINISH 1.09

C
START 5.24
FINISH 2.11

D
START 7.35
FINISH ?

E
START 6.28
FINISH 4.22

PUZZLE 102

All these bikes took part in an overnight race.
Something really weird happened! The start and finish
times of the bike became mathematically linked. If you
can discover the link you should be able to decide
when bike D finished.

See answer 16

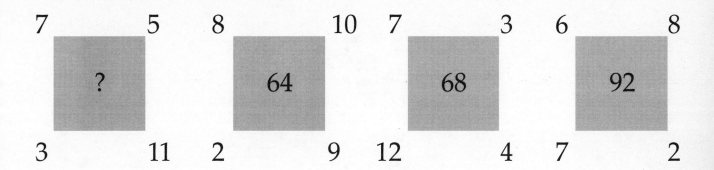

7   5   8   10   7   3   6   8

?   64   68   92

3   11   2   9   12   4   7   2

PUZZLE 103

Can you work out the reasoning behind these squares
and find the missing number?

See answer 32

PUZZLE 104

To which of these diagrams could you add a circle to
match the conditions of the above figure?

See answer 148

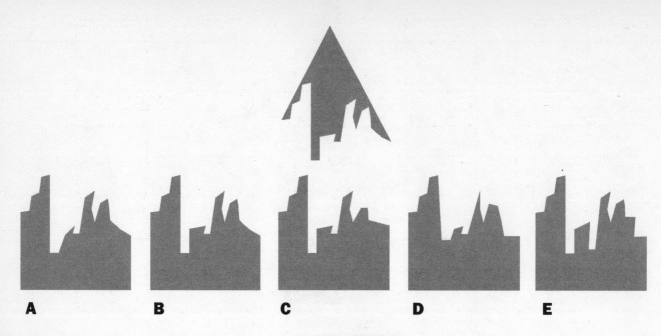

PUZZLE 105

Which of these shapes fits the above to
complete the polygon?

See answer 174

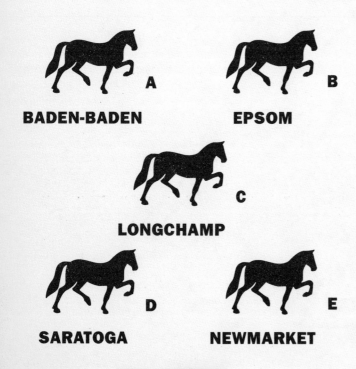

BADEN-BADEN

EPSOM

LONGCHAMP

SARATOGA

NEWMARKET

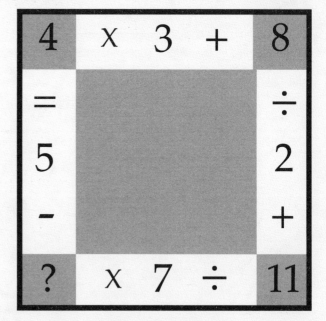

PUZZLE 106

All these horses are about to race at famous courses
around the world. Which is the odd one out?

See answer 11

PUZZLE 107

Can you replace the question mark with a number?

See answer 143

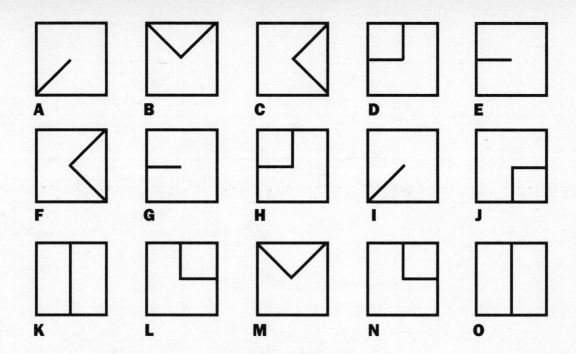

PUZZLE 108

Can you work out which of these squares is
the odd one out?

See answer 103

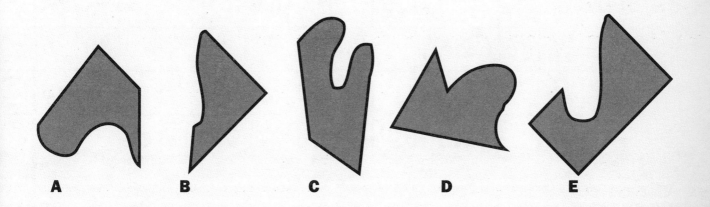

PUZZLE 109

Can you find the odd shape out?

See answer 108

&	&	%	*	%	@	@	%	*	&	&	%	*	%	@	@
*	@	@	%	*	&	&	%	*	%	@	@	%	*	&	&
%	%	&	&	%	*	%	@	@	%	*	&	&	%	*	%
@	*	*	*	%	@	@	%	*	&	&	%	*	%	%	*
@	%	%	%	@				&	&	%	*	%	@	@	%
%	&	@	&	%				&	&	%	*	@	@	@	@
*	&	@	&	*				*	&	&	%	@	%	%	@
%	*	%	*	%	%	@	@	@	%	%	@	%	*	*	%
&	%	*	%	&	*	%	%	*	*	*	@	*	&	&	*
&	@	%	@	&	%	*	%	&	&	%	%	&	&	&	&
*	@	&	@	*	&	&	*	%	@	@	*	&	%	%	&
%	%	&	%	%	@	@	%	*	%	&	&	%	*	*	%
@	*	*	*	%	&	&	*	%	@	@	%	*	%	%	*
@	%	%	@	@	%	*	%	&	&	*	%	@	@	@	%
%	&	&	*	%	@	@	%	*	%	&	&	*	%	@	@
*	%	&	&	*	%	@	@	%	*	%	&	&	*	%	@

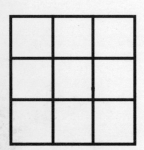

PUZZLE 110

Can you work out the pattern sequence and fill in the missing section?

See answer 101

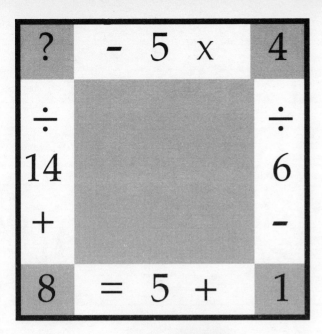

PUZZLE 111

Can you work out which number should replace the
question mark?

See answer 152

PUZZLE 112

Can you find the number that comes next
in this series?

See answer 65

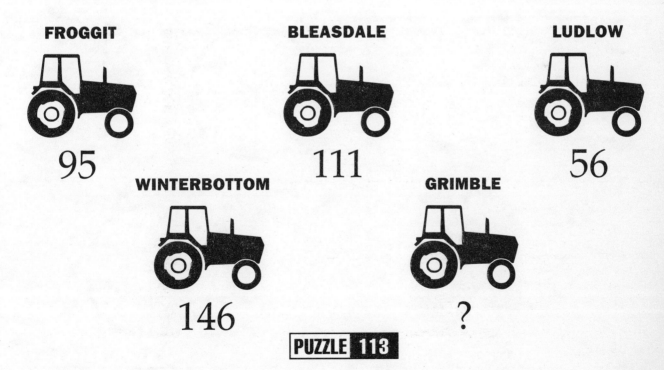

FROGGIT 95

BLEASDALE 111

LUDLOW 56

WINTERBOTTOM 146

GRIMBLE ?

PUZZLE 113

Each farmer gets a different tonnage per acre.
Somehow the tons is related to the letters in his name.
How many tons does Grimble get? You need to find
two possible values for each letter.

See answer 61

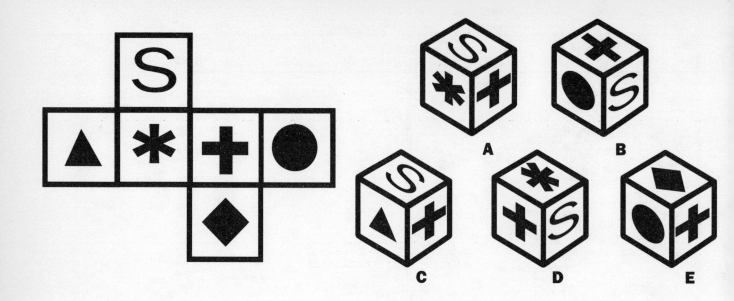

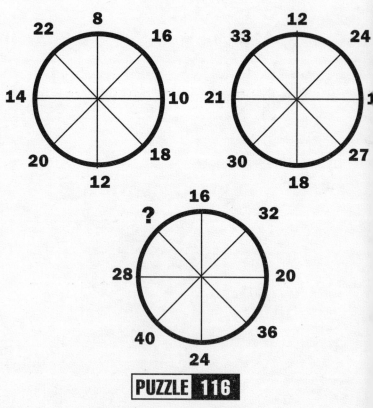

PUZZLE 114

Which cube can be made from this layout?

See answer 114

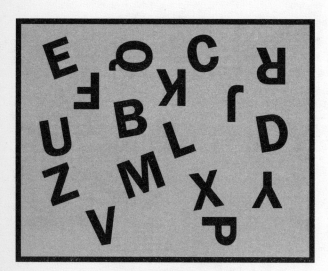

PUZZLE 115

Here is another diagam in which we have supplied the letters you do NOT need to complete the puzzle! When you have decided which letters are missing rearrange them and you will find a city named after a US President. Beware! One letter is used twice.

See answer 166

PUZZLE 116

Can you find work out which number should replace the question mark?

See answer 33

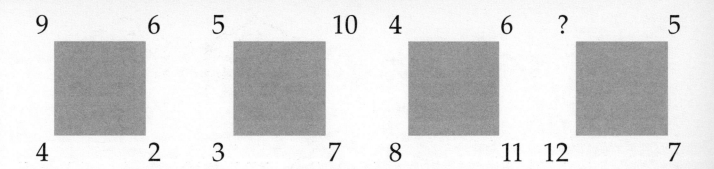

9   6   5   10   4   6   ?   5

4   2   3   7   8   11   12   7

PUZZLE 117

Can you work out the reasoning behind these
squares and find the number that should
replace the question mark?

See answer 110

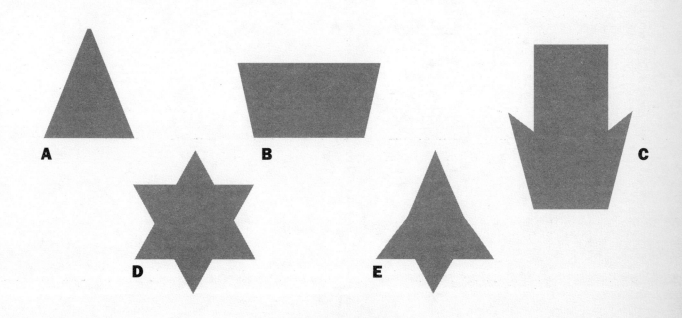

PUZZLE 118

Can you find the odd shape out?

See answer 147

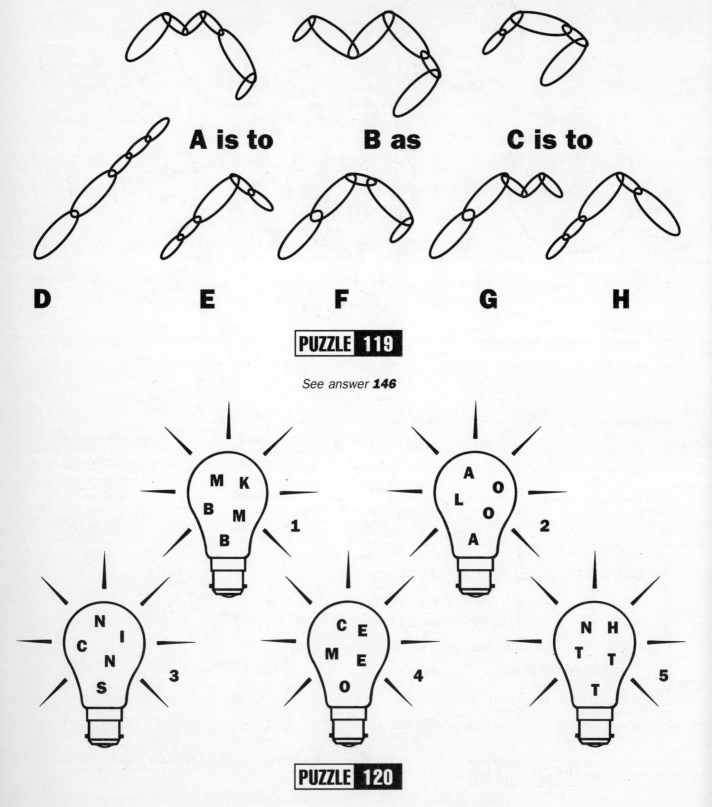

A is to   B as   C is to

D   E   F   G   H

PUZZLE 119

See answer 146

1 2 3 4 5

PUZZLE 120

Pick one letter from each bulb in order. You can make the
names of five artists.

See answer 28

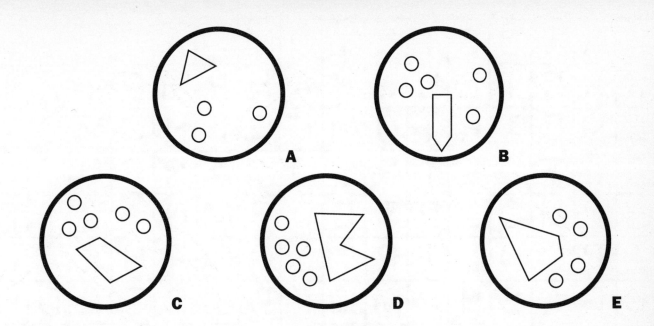

A
B
C
D
E

PUZZLE 121

Can you find the odd diagram out?

See answer 124

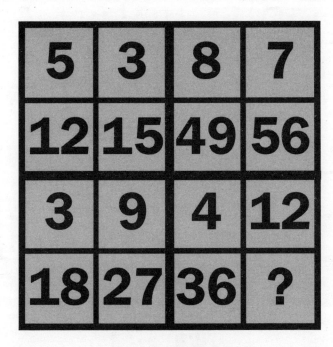

PUZZLE 122

Can you work out the reasoning behind this square
and replace the question mark with a number?

See answer 23

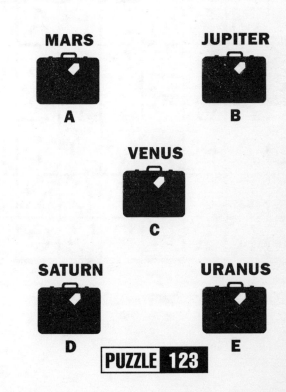

MARS — A
JUPITER — B
VENUS — C
SATURN — D
URANUS — E

PUZZLE 123

The first interplanetary travellers are about to
set off. Whose luggage is going to be put off
at the wrong stop?

See answer 49

A	R	C	D	E	T	R	I	O	M	P	A	R	C	D	E
R	R	R	T	E	D	C	R	A	H	P	M	O	I	R	T
C	D	C	T	R	I	O	M	P	H	E	H	P	M	O	I
D	E	T	D	E	T	R	I	O	M	A	R	C	D	E	A
H	P	M	O	I	R	T	E	D	P	M	O	I	R	T	R
A	R	C	D	E	T	R	I	E	O	M	P	H	E	A	R
C	R	A	E	H	P	M	T	E	D	I	R	T	E	D	C
D	E	T	R	I	O	R	M	P	H	C	E	A	R	C	D
C	D	T	R	I	I	O	M	P	H	E	R	M	I	I	E
R	A	E	H	O	P	M	O	I	R	T	P	A	R	R	T
O	M	P	M	H	E	A	R	I	D	E	H	O	T	T	R
I	R	P	T	E	D	C	R	A	E	H	E	I	E	E	I
R	H	C	D	E	T	R	I	O	M	P	A	R	D	D	O
E	A	H	P	M	O	I	R	T	E	D	R	T	A	C	M
D	E	T	R	I	O	M	P	H	A	R	C	E	R	R	P
C	R	A	H	P	M	O	I	R	T	E	D	D	C	A	H

PUZZLE 124

The phrase ARC DE TRIOMPHE is concealed
somewhere in this grid. It occurs in its entirety only
once. It is written in straight lines with only one
change of direction. Can you find it?

See answer 43

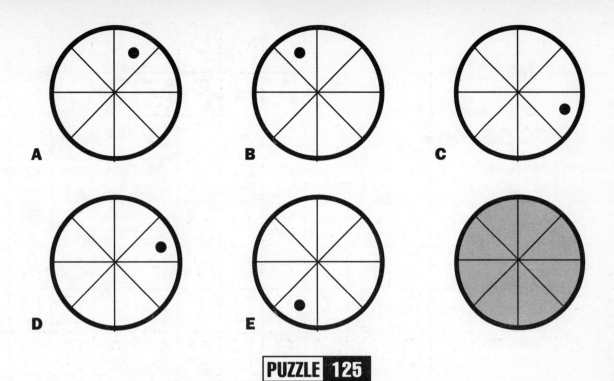

A **B** **C**

D **E**

PUZZLE 125

Can you work out what the next wheel in this sequence should look like?

See answer 55

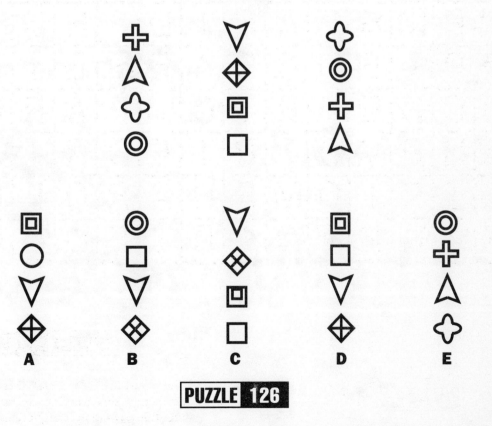

A **B** **C** **D** **E**

PUZZLE 126

Which of these columns would continue the sequence above?

See answer 130

MINNEAPOLIS
DALLAS
ANDOVER
ROCKFORD
DAVENPORT

INDEPENDENCE
WICHITA FALLS
ATLANTA
CHICAGO
PASADENA
NEW YORK

PUZZLE 127

Which of the names in the right column can be added
to the left one? This may seem confusing initially but,
despite appearances, it is not an American puzzle and
you will find a capital solution.

See answer 139

SOLAR SPRINTER   SILVER STREAK

SKY FLY

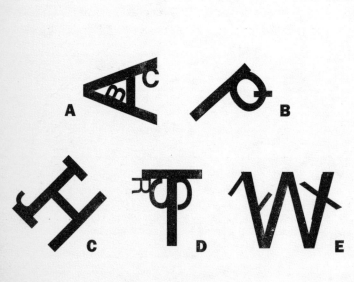

A   B

C   D   E

SUPER SAVAGE   STEEL SABER

PUZZLE 128

Can you work out which symbol is the odd one out?

See answer 125

PUZZLE 129

All these horses are ready for the off.
Which is the odd one out?

See answer 48

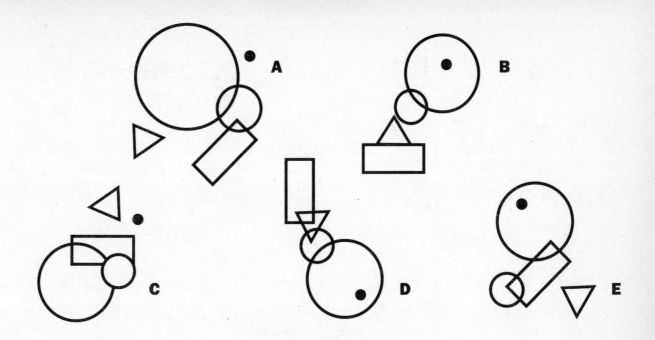

PUZZLE 130

Can you find the odd diagram out?

See answer **142**

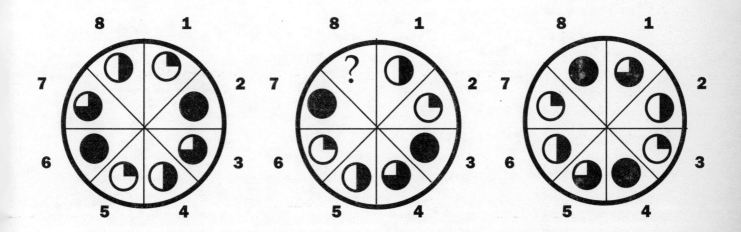

PUZZLE 131

Can you work out which shape should replace the question mark?

See answer **22**

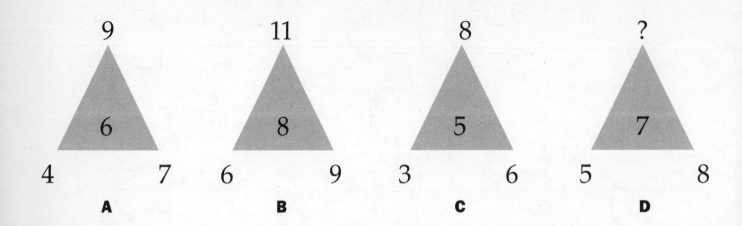

9   11   8   ?

6   8   5   7

4   7   6   9   3   6   5   8

A   B   C   D

PUZZLE 132

Can you work out the logic behind these triangles and
replace the question mark with a number?

See answer **100**

**Stephie goes on
holiday around
Europe.
She likes Hamburg
but hates Berlin.
She likes Strasbourg
but avoids Paris.
She loves Barcelona
but hates Madrid.**

Does she like London?

PUZZLE 133

See answer **157**

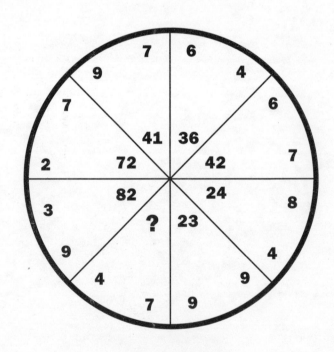

PUZZLE 134

Can you work out which number should replace the
question mark?

See answer **13**

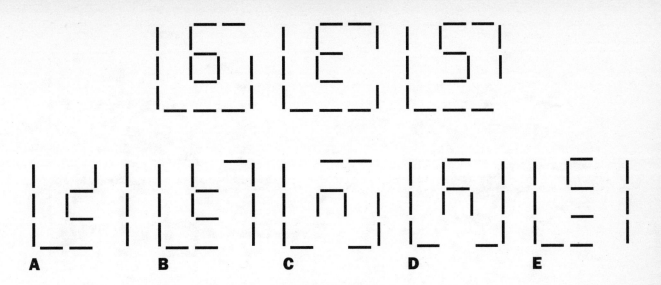

PUZZLE 135

Can you work out which of these diagrams would continue the series?

See answer 141

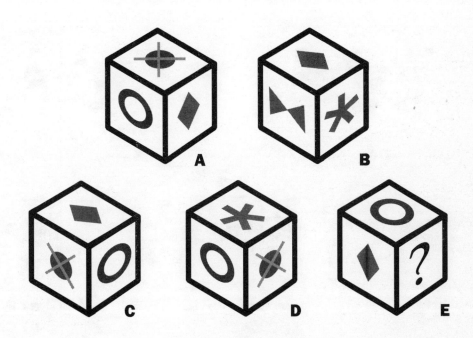

PUZZLE 136

Which of these shapes should replace the question mark?

See answer 29

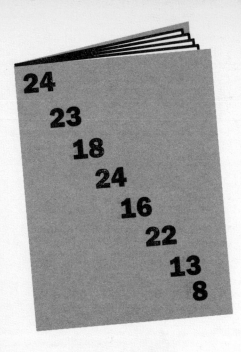

PUZZLE 137

Can you unravel the code on this book to find its famous author?

See answer 1

PUZZLE 138

Can you unravel the logic behind this square and find the missing letter?

See answer 81

A

No. 220
Denver

B

No. 47
Kansas City

C

No. 25
Galveston

D

No. 363
Lafayette

E

No. 428
a) **Portland**
b) **Chicago**
c) **Nashville**
d) **Buffalo**

PUZZLE 139

The number of each train and its destination are in some way related. Can you work out where train No. 428 is bound for?

See answer 47

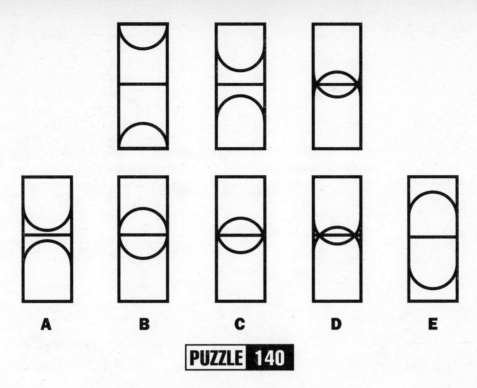

PUZZLE 140

Can you work out which of these symbols follows
the sequence above?

See answer 113

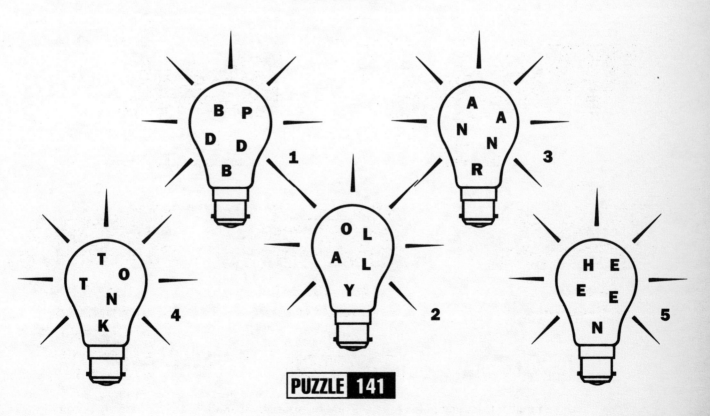

PUZZLE 141

Take one letter from each of these bulbs in order.
You will be able to make the names of five poets.

See answer 19

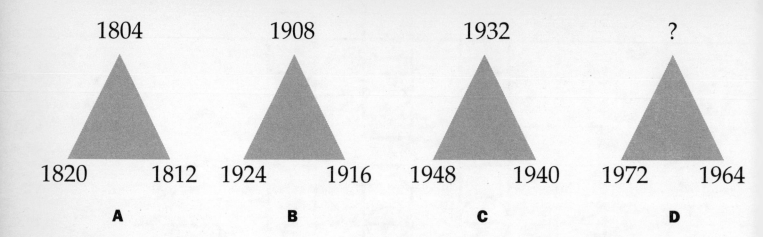

1804

1820   1812

A

1908

1924   1916

B

1932

1948   1940

C

?

1972   1964

D

PUZZLE 142

Can you work out the reasoning behind these triangles and replace the question mark with a number?

See answer 34

No. 10

Arrives 2.15

No. 2

Arrives 3.02

No. 30

Arrives 2.45

No. 8

Arrives 3.08

No. ?

Arrives 2.30

3 4 6 8 9 12 15 16 ?

PUZZLE 143

Can you find the number that comes next in this series?

See answer 66

PUZZLE 144

Five cyclists are taking part in a race. The number of each rider and its arrival time are in some way related. Can you work out the number of the rider who arrives at 2.30?

See answer 3

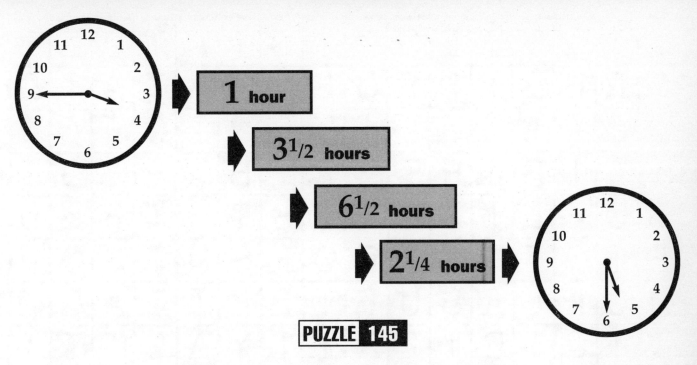

PUZZLE 145

Can you work out, using the amounts of time specified, whether you have to go forward or backward to get from the time on the top clock to the bottom clock?

See answer 162

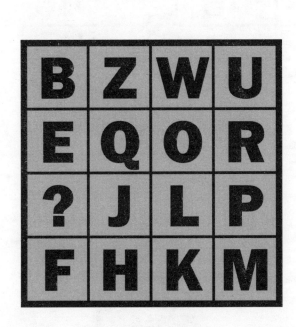

PUZZLE 146

Can you work out which letter should replace the question mark in this square?

See answer 31

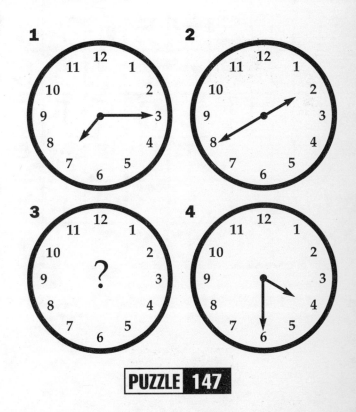

PUZZLE 147

The following clock faces are in some way related. Can you work out what the time on clock No. 3 should be?

See answer 5

S	T	A	T	U	E	O	R	T	S	T	A	T	U	E	S
S	R	E	B	I	L	F	O	E	U	T	A	T	A	T	D
L	S	T	A	T	U	L	I	B	E	R	T	O	F	F	A
I	L	I	B	E	R	T	E	L	I	B	E	R	L	O	T
B	O	F	L	I	B	U	E	O	S	T	A	I	F	S	U
E	T	S	T	A	T	U	E	O	F	S	B	T	S	O	F
R	O	F	L	A	S	U	F	T	L	E	T	T	A	S	L
T	I	C	T	B	T	L	R	I	T	Y	A	S	T	T	I
Y	U	S	E	A	I	S	B	Y	T	T	A	T	U	A	B
E	L	I	T	B	B	E	E	S	T	A	T	U	E	T	E
R	T	S	E	Y	R	Y	T	R	E	B	L	F	O	U	R
S	T	R	A	T	U	S	O	F	L	I	B	E	R	T	Y
L	T	I	S	B	E	T	O	F	S	T	A	T	U	E	O
Y	T	A	T	U	E	A	F	O	T	R	E	B	I	L	F
E	B	I	L	F	O	T	S	T	A	T	U	E	O	E	L
R	T	S	T	A	T	U	T	S	F	O	T	R	E	B	I

PUZZLE 148

The phrase STATUE OF LIBERTY is concealed in
this grid. It occurs only once in its entirety. Can you
find it? It is written in straight lines with only one
change of direction.

See answer 98

160

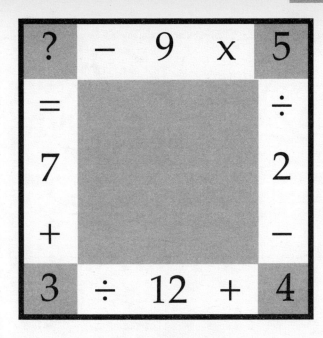

PUZZLE 149

Can you work out which number should replace the question mark in this square?

See answer 138

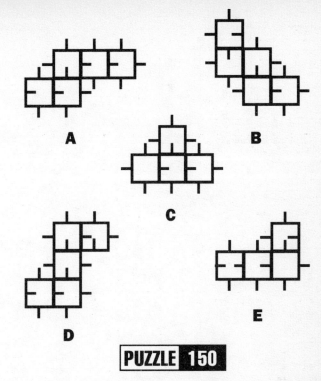

PUZZLE 150

Can you work out which diagram is the odd one out?

See answer 140

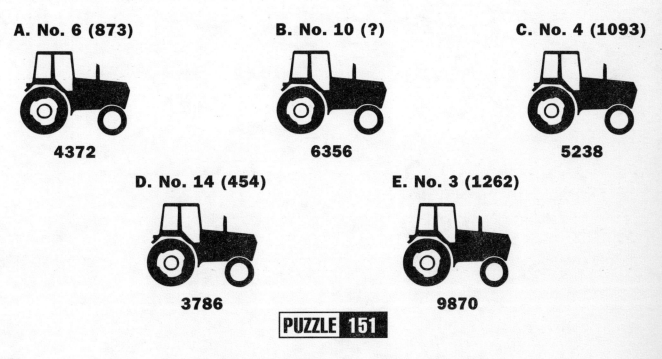

A. No. 6 (873)

4372

B. No. 10 (?)

6356

C. No. 4 (1093)

5238

D. No. 14 (454)

3786

E. No. 3 (1262)

9870

PUZZLE 151

Each tractor gathers potatoes over a certain acreage (shown in brackets). The weight of potatoes in kilos is shown under each tractor. There is a relationship between the number of the tractor, the acreage and the weight gathered. What weight should tractor B show?

See answer 39

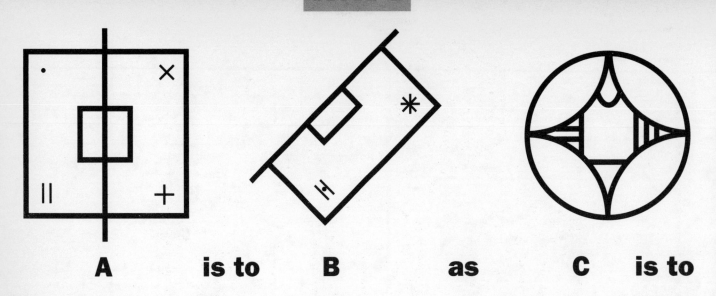

A is to **B** as **C** is to

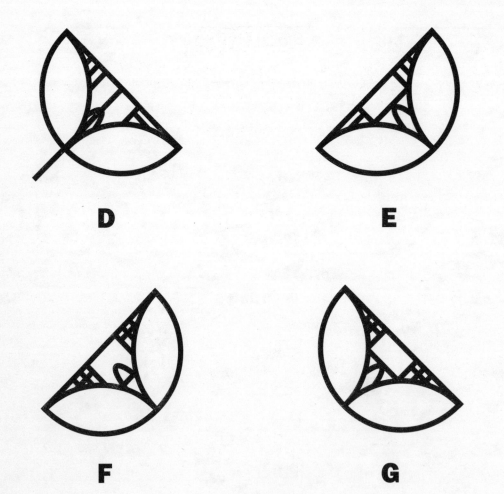

D   **E**

F   **G**

See answer 6

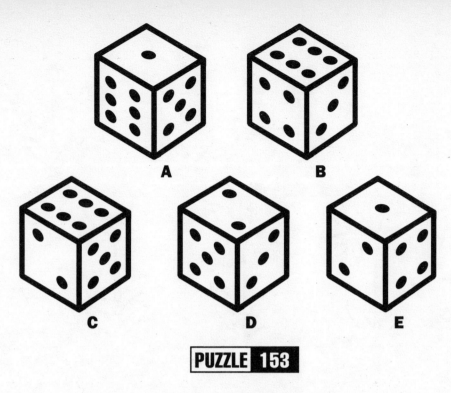

PUZZLE 153

Can you work out which of these cubes is not the same
as the others?

See answer 2

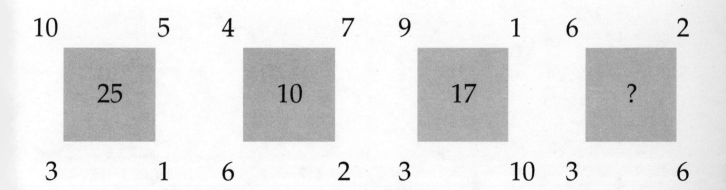

PUZZLE 154

Can you unravel the logic behind these squares and find
the missing number?

See answer 71

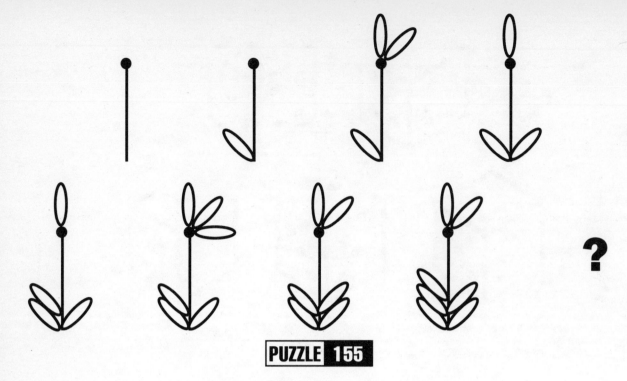

PUZZLE 155

Can you work out what the next flower in this series should look like?

See answer 95

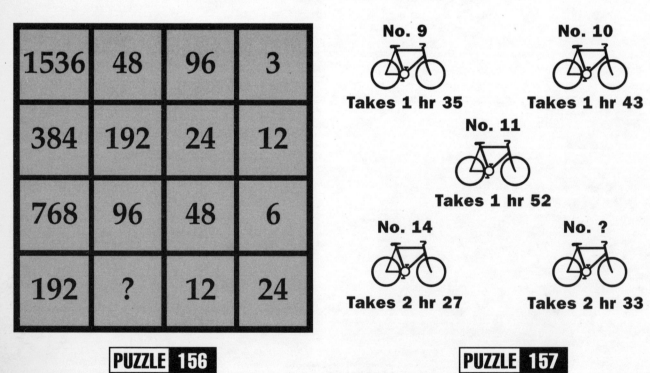

PUZZLE 156

Can you find the missing number in this square?

See answer 10

PUZZLE 157

Five cyclists are taking part in a race. The number of each rider and his cycling time are related to each other. Can you work out the number of the last cyclist?

See answer 38

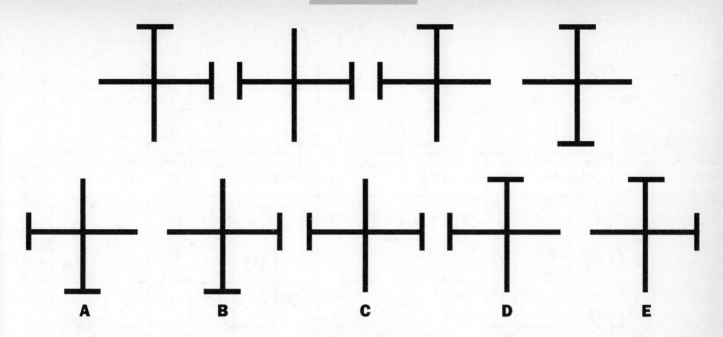

A   B   C   D   E

Can you work out which of these symbols would continue the series?

See answer **134**

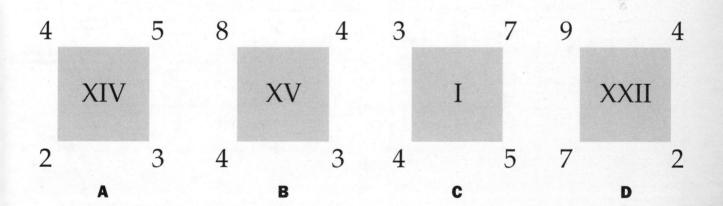

Which of these squares does not follow the same rule as the others?

See answer **74**

S	E	R	E	P	E	N	S	T	I	N	E	R	E	S	E
E	E	S	E	N	R	P	E	N	S	E	R	P	E	N	T
R	S	R	S	E	I	S	R	T	E	R	P	E	N	T	I
P	E	P	P	S	E	T	P	I	N	E	N	E	S	S	S
E	R	E	S	N	T	N	N	N	E	R	I	N	N	N	E
N	P	N	E	R	T	E	T	E	P	N	S	E	E	I	R
T	E	T	R	P	S	I	I	T	P	T	P	T	R	T	P
N	N	I	P	E	E	N	N	T	R	R	S	E	P	N	E
E	T	N	E	N	T	E	E	E	E	S	E	T	E	E	N
I	N	E	N	T	R	S	E	S	R	E	T	S	N	P	T
S	E	R	T	P	E	N	T	I	N	E	T	S	T	R	I
S	E	R	N	P	E	N	T	I	N	E	E	N	I	E	T
E	S	R	E	I	S	E	R	P	E	N	T	I	N	S	E
S	E	T	E	N	N	I	T	N	E	P	R	E	S	T	E
R	S	E	N	E	I	T	N	I	P	R	E	S	E	S	T
S	E	R	P	E	N	S	N	I	T	N	E	P	R	E	S

PUZZLE 160

The word SERPENTINE is hidden somewhere in this grid. It occurs in its entirety only once. Can you find it? It may be spelt in any direction but is all in one line.

See answer 59

PUZZLE 161

Pick one letter from each cloud in order. You should be able to make the names of five Roman emperors.

See answer 63

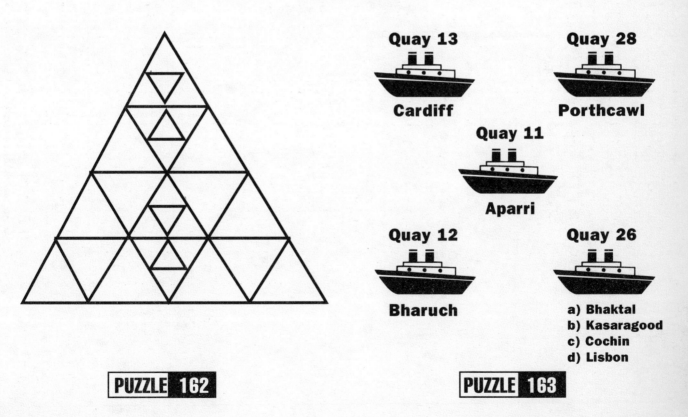

PUZZLE 162

PUZZLE 163

Can you work out how many triangles there are in this diagram altogether?

See answer 99

The number of the quay and the ship's destination are in some way related. Can you work out which harbour the ship on Quay 26 is bound for?

See answer 4

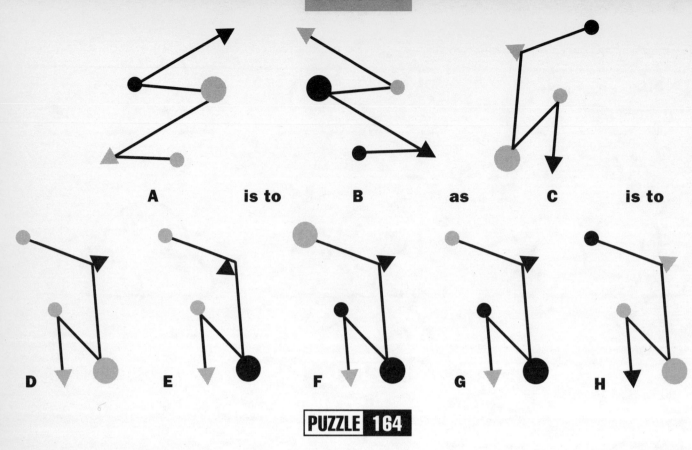

A   is to   B   as   C   is to

PUZZLE 164

See answer 112

16	10	20	14
8	140	134	28
14	70	268	22
7	?	38	44

PUZZLE 165

Can you find the number to replace the question mark?

See answer 27

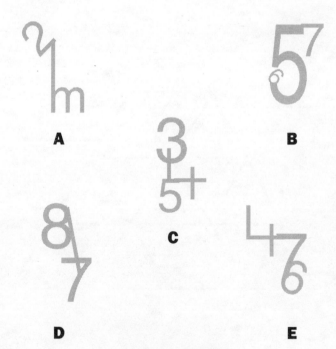

PUZZLE 166

Can you find the odd figure out?

See answer 132

PUZZLE 167

Can you find the shape that should replace the question mark in the last circle?

See answer 8

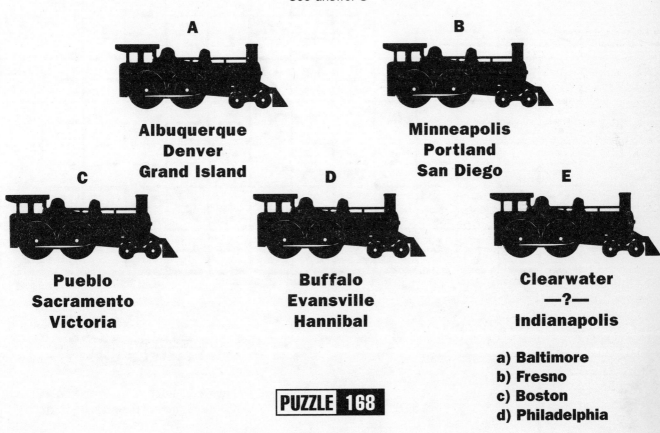

A
Albuquerque
Denver
Grand Island

B
Minneapolis
Portland
San Diego

C
Pueblo
Sacramento
Victoria

D
Buffalo
Evansville
Hannibal

E
Clearwater
—?—
Indianapolis

a) Baltimore
b) Fresno
c) Boston
d) Philadelphia

PUZZLE 168

These trains pass three American towns on their route. Can you find the missing town of the last train?
See answer 37

This grid follows a certain pattern. Can you work out which signs complete the missing grid?

See answer 70

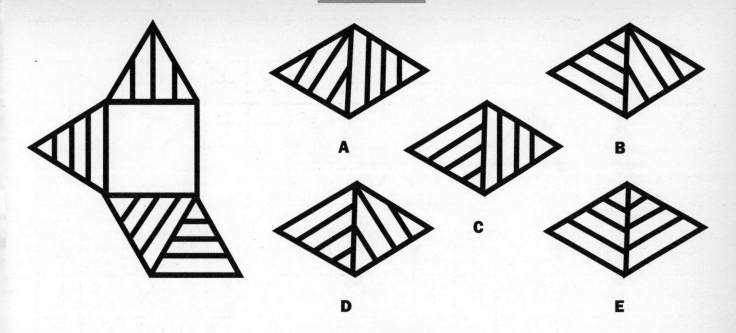

A

B

C

D

E

PUZZLE 170

Can you work out which two pyramids cannot be made
from the above layout?

See answer 168

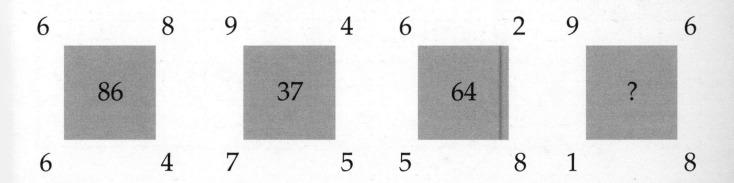

6	8	9	4	6	2	9	6

| 86 | 37 | 64 | ? |

| 6 | 4 | 7 | 5 | 5 | 8 | 1 | 8 |

PUZZLE 171

Can you work out the reasoning behind these squares and
replace the question mark with a number?

See answer 72

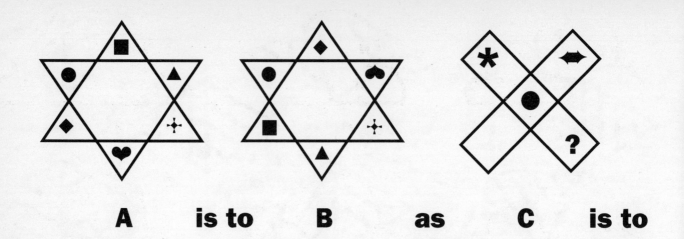

A   is to   B   as   C   is to

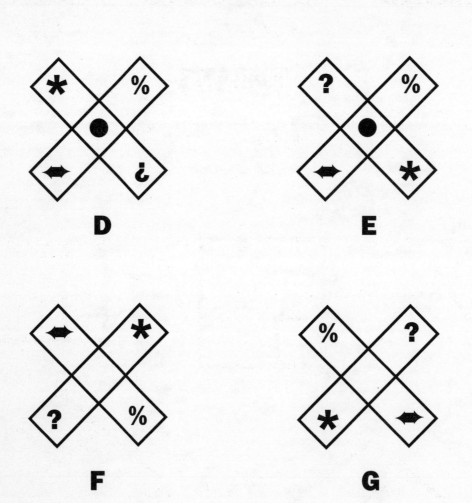

D

E

F

G

PUZZLE 173

Take one letter from each cloud in order. You should be
able to make the names of five playwrights.

See answer 25

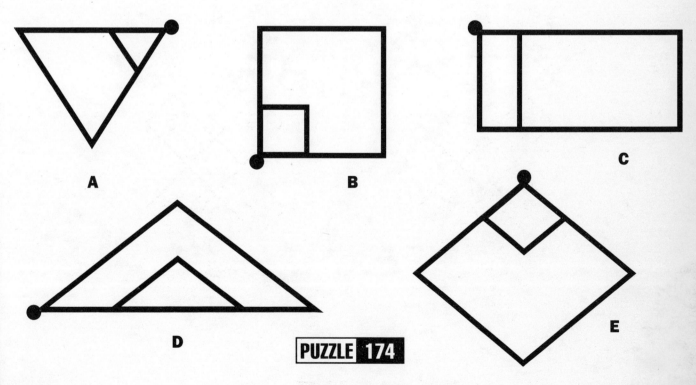

PUZZLE 174

Can you find the odd shape out?

See answer 133

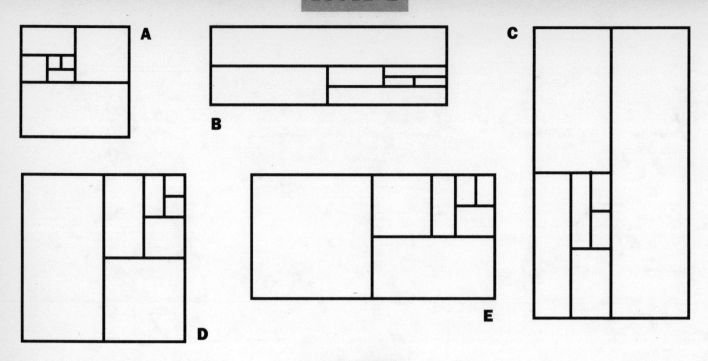

PUZZLE 175

Can you work out which of these diagrams is the odd one out?

See answer 107

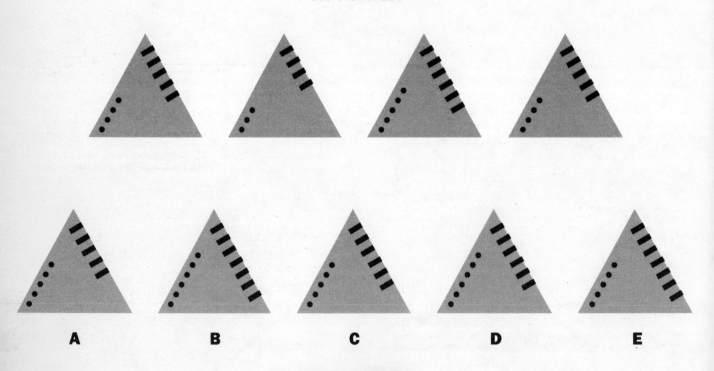

PUZZLE 176

Can you find the symbol that would continue the sequence above?

See answer 126

PUZZLE 177

Can you work out what the next symbol in this sequence should look like?

See answer 44

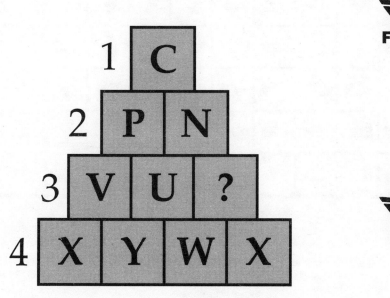

PUZZLE 178

Can you find the letter which completes this diagram?

See answer 14

Quay 28 — Felixstowe

Quay 37 — Durban

Quay 58 — Cape Town

Quay 27 — Eureka

Quay 89

a) Long Beach
b) East London
c) Alexander Bay
d) Lagos

PUZZLE 179

Can you work out where the boat leaving from Quay 89 is bound for?

See answer 24

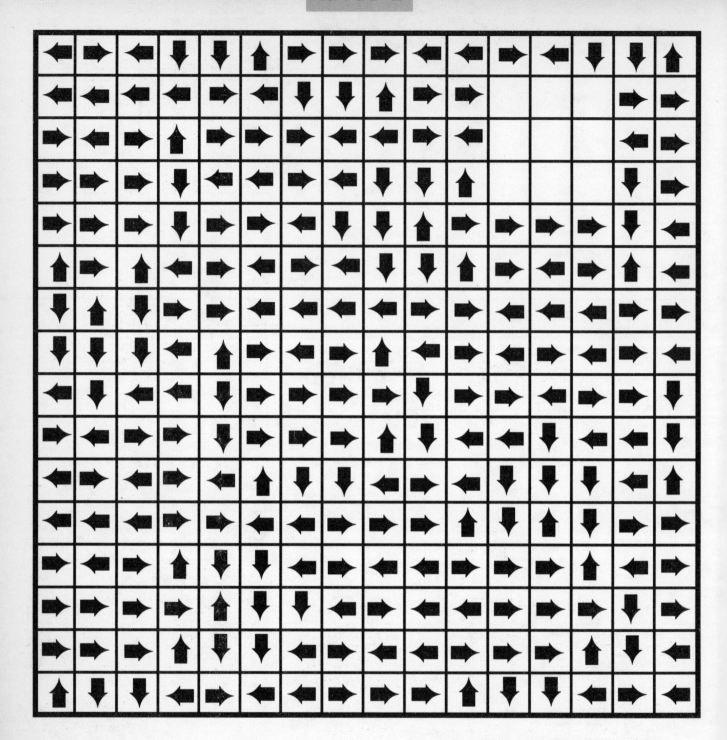

PUZZLE 180

This grid is made up according to a pattern. Can you work it out and complete the missing section?

*See answer **12***

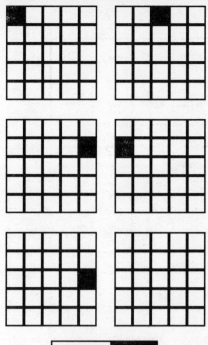

11 13 17 25 32 37 47 ?

PUZZLE 181

Can you work out which number comes next in this series?

See answer 82

PUZZLE 182

Can you work out where the shaded square in the last diagram should be?

See answer 129

Die Zeit

1216124

Boston Globe

13443323311

Daily Mail

112353123

France Soir

2413114324

Ethnos

?

PUZZLE 183

Each balloon has been sponsored by a famous newspaper and given a registration number based on the paper's name. What number should the *Ethnos* balloon bear?

See answer 17

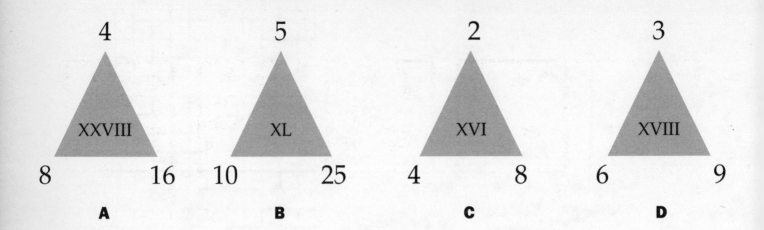

PUZZLE 184

Can you work out which triangle does not follow the same rule as the others?

See answer 73

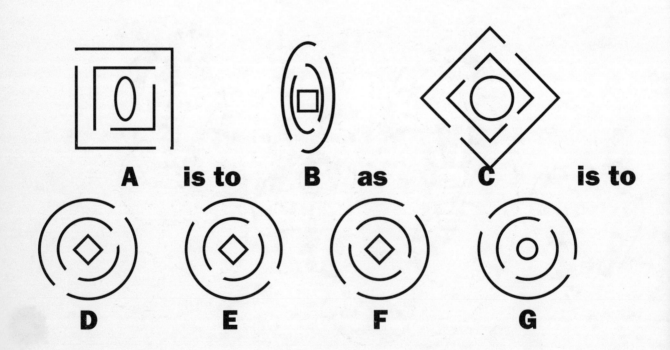

PUZZLE 185

See answer 89

A   B   C   D   E

PUZZLE 186

Can you find the odd diagram out?

See answer 127

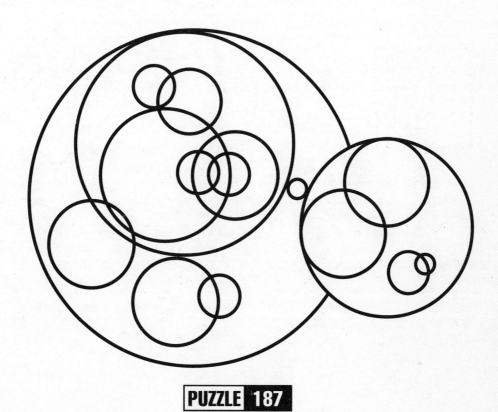

PUZZLE 187

How many circles can you find in this diagram altogether?

See answer 76

Answer 1
C. Dickens. The code is based on the number alphabet reversed, i.e. Z = 1, A = 26, etc.

Answer 2
C.

Answer 3
20. Multiply hours by minutes and divide by 3 to get the number of the rider.

Answer 4
D. Multiply digits. The resulting product gives the alphabetical position of the first letter of the place name.

Answer 5
9.05. The minute hand goes forward 25 minutes, the hour hand back by 5 hours.

Answer 6
E. Fold the top half onto the bottom half and turn the shape 45° anti-clockwise.

Answer 7
Carmen, Fidelio, La Traviata, Lohengrin, Boris Godunov. The additional opera is Don Giovanni.

Answer 8
 The symbols are determined by the number of sides, as follows: circle 1, L-shape 2, triangle 3, square 4, pentagon 5, hexagon 6. Starting at 1 and moving in a clockwise direction skip 1 shape, then 2, repeat. When you have reached the 8th segment continue with the 1st segment in the 2nd circle, and continue in the same order in this and the subsequent circle.

Answer 9
The shapes form two series which go from top to bottom of succeeding squares. The squares and circles alternate. The sequence of shading is: quarter, half, three-quarters, fully shaded.

Answer 10
384. Starting at the top right hand corner work through the square in a vertical boustrophedon, multiplying by 4 and dividing by 2 alternately.

Answer 11
D. They are all in alphabetical order except for D.

Answer 12
It starts at the top left and works inward in an anti-clockwise spiral.

Answer 13
18. Multiply the numbers in the outer section, reverse the product and put in the middle of the next section.

Answer 14
T. Based on the number alphabet backwards, add together two consecutive squares in the same row. Convert the sum to a new letter and put in the row above in the square that is directly above the two consecutive squares.

Answer 15
No. 2. Take the first digit of the weight from the second to arrive at new number.

Answer 16
3.13. Start time A minus Finish A = Finish B. Start time B minus Finish B = Finish C, etc.

Answer 17
142334. It works on a number code. 1 is letters A–E inclusive, 2 F–J, 3 K–O, 4 P–T, 5 U–Y and 6 Z.

Answer 18
Denver, Buffalo, Saginaw, Boston, Seattle, Miami. The extra city is Philadelphia.

Answer 19
Blake, Byron, Dante, Donne, Plath.

Answer 20
G. It is a term for tempo, while the others are types of dances.

Answer 21
Ratatouille. It is the only vegetarian dish.

Answer 22

The sequence is:

The symbol moves from section 1 in the first circle to section 1 in the second circle, then to section 1 in the third circle, and then to section 2 in the first circle etc.

Answer 23

48. In each box of four numbers, multiply the top two numbers, put the product in the bottom right box, then subtract the top right number from the bottom right one and put the difference in the bottom left box.

Answer 24

C. Take the first digit from the second. The resulting digit gives the alphabetic number of the initial letter of the answer.

Answer 25

Brecht, Coward, Dryden, Pinter, Racine.

Answer 26

21. △ = 12, ✳ = 9, ♡ = 3, % = 5, @ = 7.

Answer 27

76. Starting at the bottom left hand corner, work through the square in a clockwise spiral, multiplying by 2 and subtracting 6, alternately.

Answer 28

Bacon, Bosch, Klimt, Manet, Monet.

Answer 29

A.

Answer 30

Camus, Defoe, Dumas, Verne, Wells.

Answer 31

G. Starting at the bottom left corner, work through the alphabet in an anti-clockwise spiral. Miss 1 letter, then 2 letters, 1 letter, etc., going back to the start of the alphabet after reaching Z.

Answer 32

92. Multiply the numbers on the diagonally opposite corners of each square and add the products. Put the sum in the third square along.

Answer 33

44. The numbers increase clockwise first missing one spoke, then two at the fourth step. Each circle increases by a different amount (2, 3, 4).

Answer 34

1956. The numbers represent the leap years clockwise around the triangles starting at the apex. Miss one leap year each time.

Answer 35

Tiramisu. This is a dessert; the others are all main courses.

Answer 36

Add the number of segments in column 1 to the number of segments in column 3. Draw this number of segments in to column 2.

Answer 37

Fresno. Skip two letters in the alphabet each time.

Answer 38

15. Take the minutes in the hours, add the minutes and divide by 10. Ignore the remainder.

Answer 39

987. The tractor number is divided into the weight to give the acreage. The weights have been mixed up.

Answer 40

Kebab, Pasta, Pizza, Tacos, Wurst.

Answer 41

Bartok, Boulez, Chopin, Delius, Mahler.

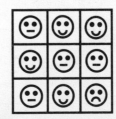

Answer 42

The faces pattern sequence is smiley, smiley, straight, sad, sad, smiley, straight, straight, sad, etc. Start at the bottom left and work in a horizontal boustrophedon.

Answer 43

A	R	C	D	E	T	R	I	O	M	P	A	R	C	D	E
R	R	R	T	E	D	C	R	A	H	P	M	O	I	R	T
C	D	C	T	R	I	O	M	P	H	E	H	P	M	O	I
D	E	T	D	E	T	R	I	O	M	A	R	C	D	E	A
H	P	M	O	I	R	T	E	D	P	M	O	I	R	T	R
A	R	C	D	E	T	R	I	E	O	M	P	H	E	A	R
C	R	A	E	H	P	M	T	E	D	I	R	T	E	D	C
D	E	T	R	I	O	R	M	P	H	C	E	A	R	C	D
C	D	T	R	I	I	O	M	P	H	E	R	M	I	I	E
R	A	E	H	O	P	M	O	I	R	T	P	A	R	R	T
O	M	P	M	H	E	A	R	I	D	E	H	O	T	T	R
I	R	P	T	E	D	C	R	A	E	H	E	I	E	E	I
R	H	C	D	E	T	R	I	O	M	P	A	R	D	D	O
E	A	H	P	M	O	I	R	T	E	D	R	T	A	C	M
D	E	T	R	I	O	M	P	H	A	R	C	E	R	R	P
C	R	A	H	P	M	O	I	R	T	E	D	D	C	A	H

Answer 44

The symbol turns 180° clockwise, 135° anti-clockwise, 90° clockwise, 45° anti-clockwise.

Answer 45

♡ = 8, ♣ = 4, ◇ = 6, ♠ = 2.

Answer 46

Idaho, Iowa, Maine, Texas, Utah. The dummy letters are K and L.

Answer 47

C. Add the digits to get the alphabetic number of the town's initial letter.

Answer 48

Sky Fly. The name contains no vowels.

Answer 49

C. The others are all in the correct order if you start from Earth and travel away from the sun.

Answer 50

Bodega, Bonsai, Ersatz, Hombre, Kitsch.

3	3	2
2	3	4
3	2	1

Answer 51

The pattern sequence is 1, 2, 2, 3, 4, 4, 1, 2, 3, 3, 4. Start at the top left and work in a horizontal boustrophedon.

Answer 52
The pattern is +2 scales, +3 scales, −1 scale. A fish with an even number of scales faces the other way.

Answer 53
The pattern is +1 limb, +2, +3, −2, −1, +1, +2, +3, etc. A figure with an uneven number of limbs is turned upside down.

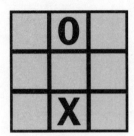

Answer 54
Starting at opposite ends the symbols move alternately 1 and 2 steps to the other end of the grid in a boustrophedon.

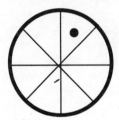

Answer 55
Starting with a vertical line reflect the dot first against that line and then each following line in a clockwise direction.

Answer 56
21.

Answer 57
The corresponding sections in each wheel should contain a black section in each compartment.

Answer 58
Brunel, Darwin, Edison, Pascal, Planck.

Answer 59 – See page 184

Answer 60
D. All the others are cities, Kansas is a state (Kansas City actually straddles the Missouri-Kansas border).

Answer 61
61. Letters are worth the value based on alphabetical position (A=1, etc.). However, alternate letters are worth the value based on the reversed alphabet (A=26, etc.).

Answer 62
C. Starting at the top right hand corner, work through the alphabet, missing 1, 2, 3, 4, 5, 4, 3, 2, 1, 2, etc. letters each time, in a vertical boustrophedon.

Answer 63
Gallus, Jovian, Julian, Trajan, Valens.

Answer 64
M. These are all the letters with straight sides only.

Answer 65
64. Take each digit individually. The pattern is 1, 2, 3, 1, then 2, 3, 4, 2, then 3, 4, 5, 3, and finally 4, 5, 6, 4.

Answer 66
18. These are all the numbers that can be divided by either 3 or 4.

Answer 67
B. The digits of all the others add up to 6.

Answer 68
1980. Vowels = 243, Consonants = 126

Answer 69
576. Multiply No. by speed, put the product as the distance for the next balloon.

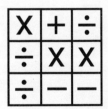

Answer 70
The pattern is:

+ + − − − ÷ ÷ X X X

Start at the top left and work clockwise in an inward spiral.

Answer 71
6. In each square, multiply the top and bottom left together, then multiply the top and bottom right. Subtract this second product from the first and put this number in the middle.

Answer 59

S	E	R	E	P	E	N	S	T	I	N	E	R	E	S	E
E	E	S	E	N	R	P	E	N	S	E	R	P	E	N	T
R	S	R	S	E	I	S	R	T	E	R	P	E	N	T	I
P	E	P	P	S	E	T	P	I	N	E	N	E	S	S	S
E	R	E	S	N	T	N	N	N	E	R	I	N	N	N	E
N	P	N	E	R	T	E	T	E	P	N	S	E	E	I	R
T	E	T	R	P	S	I	I	T	P	T	P	T	R	T	P
N	N	I	P	E	E	N	N	T	R	R	S	E	P	N	E
E	T	N	E	N	T	E	E	E	E	S	E	T	E	E	N
I	N	E	N	T	R	S	E	S	R	E	T	S	N	P	T
S	E	R	T	P	E	N	T	I	N	E	T	S	T	R	I
S	E	R	N	P	E	N	T	I	N	E	E	N	I	E	T
E	S	R	E	I	S	E	R	P	E	N	T	I	N	S	E
S	E	T	E	N	N	I	T	N	E	P	R	E	S	T	E
R	S	E	N	E	I	T	N	I	P	R	E	S	E	S	T
S	E	R	P	E	N	S	N	I	T	N	E	P	R	E	S

Answer 72

75. In each square, multiply the top and bottom left numbers, then the top and bottom right. Add these two products, reverse the digits of this sum and place it in the middle.

Answer 73

C. Divide the left number by 2, place this number at the apex, then square it and put this number at the right. Finally, add all three numbers together and put the sum as a roman numeral in the middle. In triangle C, the right number should be 4 and the middle number should be X.

Answer 74

B. In each square multiply the two top numbers, then the two bottom ones. Subtract the latter product from the former, translate the difference into Roman numerals and put it in the middle. Square B should be XX (20).

Answer 75

R. Starting on the top left hand corner, work through the alphabet, missing a letter each time, in a vertical boustrophedon.

Answer 76

17.

Answer 77
JOL 1714. Go 5 forward and 3 back in the alphabet. The numbers continue from the alphabetic position of the letter.

Answer 78
35226252257. The numbers are in code from the newspaper titles. A–C = 1, D–F = 2, G–I = 3, J–L = 4, M–O = 5, P–R = 6 S–U = 7, V–X = 8, Y–Z = 9.

Answer 79
No. 52. Add together the value of the letters based on their alphabet position.

Answer 80
29. Add together the corner squares of each row or column in a clockwise direction. Put the sum in the middle of the next row or column.

Answer 81
F. This is based on the number alphabet backwards. Add together the corner squares of each row or column and put the sum in the middle square of the opposite row or column.

Answer 82
58. Add the digits of the last number and move on by that number.

Answer 83
D. Reflect the shape along a horizontal line, then move each sign one segment clockwise.

Answer 84
QUS 2321. Go forward by 4 and back by 2 in the alphabet, then continue with numbers taken from the letters' alphabetical position.

Answer 85
No 201. Add together the values of the letters based on their reversed alphabetical position, (A = 26, Z = 1).

Answer 86
E. The shape has been folded along a horizontal line. A shaded piece covers an unshaded one.

Answer 87
Picasso. Based on the letters' position in the alphabet, 3 has been added to each value.

Answer 88
G. Add 3 to odd numbers, subtract 2 from even numbers.

Answer 89
E. The outer shape changes to the inner shape, the openings rotate through 90° clockwise.

Answer 90
84. Multiply the hours of A by the minutes of B to get the tonnage of C, then B hours by C minutes to get D, C hours by D minutes to get E, D hours by E minutes to get A, and E hours by A minutes to get the tonnage of B.

Answer 91
I. It is based on the number alphabet backwards. Add the top and bottom rows together and put the sum in the middle.

Answer 92
It should have two dots. Add together the corner squares of each row or column and put the sum in the middle square of the opposite row or column.

Answer 93
E. Based on the position of the letters in the alphabet, multiply column one by column three and place the product in the middle column.

Answer 94
D. Add consecutive clockwise corners of the diamond and place the sum on the corresponding second corner. Add the four numbers together and place the sum in the middle.

Answer 95
Add one leaf. Add two petals. Deduct 1 petal and add 1 leaf. Repeat.

Answer 98

```
S T A T U E O R T S T A T U E S
S R E B I L F O E U T A T A T D
L S T A T U L I B E R T O F F A
I L I B E R T E L I B E R L O T
B O F L I B U E O S T A I F S U
E T S T A T U E O F S B T S O F
R O F L A S U F T L E T T A S L
T I C T B T L R I T Y A S T T I
Y U S E A I S B Y T T A T U A B
E L I T B B E E S T A T U E T E
R T S E Y R Y T R E B L F O U R
S T R A T U S O F L I B E R T Y
L T I S B E T O F S T A T U E O
Y T A T U E A F O T R E B I L F
E B I L F O T S T A T U E O E L
R T S T A T U T S F O T R E B I
```

Answer 96
Renoir. The letters in this code come one before in the alphabet, with the artist's name reversed.

Answer 97
16.

Answer 98 – See above

Answer 99
3G.

Answer 100
10. Add 2 to each value, place sum in corresponding position in next triangle, then subtract 3, add 2 again.

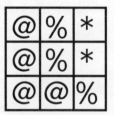

Answer 101
The pattern sequence is @, @, %, *, %, &, &, *, %. It starts at the top right and works inwards in an anti-clockwise spiral.

Answer 102
Degas. Each letter is the same number of letters from the end of the alphabet as the letter in the artist's name is from the beginning.

Answer 103
J. All of the others have a matching partner.

Answer 104
D. Alternate between rotating the pattern 90° anti-clockwise, and swapping direction of each individual arrow.

Answer 105
A. Each ring contains one cross more than the previous example, and the first and last cross in each adjacent circle are level.

Answer 106
G. The top and bottom elements swap position, the smaller central element becomes smaller still and all three elements move inside the larger central shape.

Answer 107
E. Each shape is divided into smaller ones by alternating between adding horizontal and vertical lines (or vice versa) except in 'E' where 2 vertical lines are added in succession.

Answer 108
E. All elements consist of 3 straight lines except 'E' which consists of 4 straight lines.

Answer 109
C. Convert each letter to its value based on its position in the alphabet. The values on each corner of a triangle added together result in the new letter in the middle.

Answer 110
9. The numbers rotate clockwise and increase by 1 each time.

Answer 111
12. Add together the values in the same segments in wheels 1 and 3 and put the answer in the opposite segment in wheel 2.

Answer 112
G. The figures are vertical images of each other but with shaded and unshaded elements becoming unshaded and shaded respectively.

Answer 113
B. Each arch moves closer to its opposite end by an equal amount each time.

Answer 114
B.

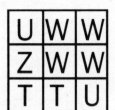

Answer 115
The pattern sequence is:

Z R T T U W W Z Z S

Start at the bottom right and work up in a horizontal boustrophedon.

Answer 116
B.

Answer 117
F. A curve turns into a straight line and a straight line into a curve.

Answer 118
A.

Answer 119
V. The letters are based on the number alphabet backwards (Z = 1, A = 26, etc). The values on the bottom corners and the value in the middle added together result in the value on the apex.

Answer 120
3. The numbers rotate anti-clockwise from one square to the next and decrease by 2 each time.

Answer 121
9. Multiply the values in the same segments in wheels 2 and 3 and put the answer in the next segment in wheel 1, going clockwise.

Answer 122
N. Going from the top to the bottom of one domino piece, then to the top of the next piece, etc., alternately move on five letters and three back.

Answer 123
T. Hardy. Each letter in this code follows that of the author, e.g. 'U' comes after 'T' in the alphabet.

Answer 124

C. The number of small circles equals the number of edges of the shape, except for 'C' where there is one more circle than edges.

Answer 125

E. All the others consist of 3 consecutive letters in the alphabet.

Answer 126

B. Deduct one dot and one line, add two dots and two lines, repeat.

Answer 127

E. All the others contain two stars for every half moon.

Answer 128

C.

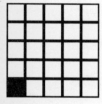

Answer 129

The shaded square moves around the square in a horizontal boustrophedon, starting at the top left hand corner. It advances by 2 squares, then 3, then 4, etc.

Answer 130

D. Each column of elements alternates and moves up two rows.

Answer 131

J. Austen. Each number is double the letters' alphabetical position.

Answer 132

E. All the other elements consist of 3 consecutive numbers.

Answer 133

D. The circle in all other elements intercepts an edge in both the small and large shape outline.

Answer 134

A. Each small bar moves one place anti-clockwise in alternate shapes, so that they are either 90° or 180° apart.

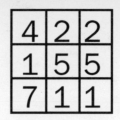

Answer 135

The pattern sequence is 7, 1, 1, 3, 2, 2, 5, 5, 4, 1. It starts at the top right and works in an anti-clockwise spiral.

Answer 136

+ ÷ − X − +. The letters are based on their alphabetic position, so the sum would read:
L(12) **+** D(4) **÷** B(2) **−** F(6) **X** K(11) **−** Q(17) **+** C(3) = H(8).

Answer 137

8. The sum of hands on each clock is 13.

Answer 138

13.

Answer 139

Independence. The initials can be rearranged to form the name Madrid.

Answer 140

B. It is the only figure that does not have three boxes in one row.

Answer 141

B. Working in an anti-clockwise spiral pattern, in the first square there are eight lines, one missing, seven lines, one missing, etc. The number of lines before the first break decreases by one with each square.

Answer 142

E. It is the only one where the small and large circles do not overlap.

Answer 143

3.

Answer 144

4.

Answer 145

B. It is the only figure which, with an additional line, has a triangle adjoining the rectangle which overlaps the square.

Answer 146
F. The small and large elements become large and small respectively.

Answer 147
A. It is the only one to have an odd number of lines.

Answer 148
D. It is the only one to which a circle can be added where the triangle overlaps the circle and a right angled line runs parallel to the whole of one side of the triangle.

Answer 149
B.

Answer 150
B. Each time the square becomes the circle, the triangle the square and the circle the triangle.

Answer 151
21. Multiply each number by the number on the opposite side of the wheel on the same side of the spoke and put the product in that segment next to the centre.

Answer 152
2.

Answer 153
C. It is the only one to have an odd number of one element.

Answer 154
D. A circle becomes a square, a line a circle and a square a line, all in the same size and position as original.

Answer 155
D. All the others are symmetrical.

Answer 156
F. The circles and squares become squares and circles respectively. The largest element loses all internal elements.

Answer 157
No. She hates capital cities.

Answer 158
No. Illinois had an S in it.

Answer 159
Yes. Swansea had no O in it.

Answer 160
D. The number of edges of the shapes in each square increases by 1 in each column, starting from the top.

Answer 161
E. Add two circles and two lines, take away one of each, repeat. The pattern is also rotated by 90° anti-clockwise each time.

Answer 162
Forward, back, forward, back.

Answer 163
D.

Answer 164
The pattern sequence is: 1.00, 2.00, 2.00, 1.00, 3.00, 3.00, 2.00, 4.00, 4.00. 3.00, 5.00, 5.00, 4.00, 6.00, 6.00. Starting at the bottom left work upwards in a vertical boustrophedon.

Answer 165
E.

Answer 166
Washington.

Answer 167
C.

Answer 168
D and **E**.

Answer 169

B. It consists of 14 straight lines, the rest of 13.

Answer 170

C. It is the only one which does not have half as many 'step' lines as there are triangles.

Answer 171

Pantagruel.

Answer 172

Frankenstein.

Answer 173

E. A square becomes a circle, a circle a triangle and a triangle a square of similar proportions and positions.

Answer 174

B.

Answer 175

A. Each shape increases by one of the same until there are three and it then becomes one. The image is reflected after a shape with two elements.

Answer 176

Excalibur.

Answer 177

Nostradamus.

Answer 178

H. Longer rectangles and arrows swap shading. Smaller rectangles and arrows interchange shape and shading. The pattern is then flipped vertically.

Answer 179

B. It is the only one with the same number of vertical and horizontal lines.

Answer 180

E. Two letters following the first example, facing the correct direction, run into each other.

Answer 181

D.

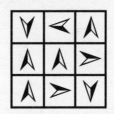

Answer 182

The pattern sequence is as follows.

Start at the bottom left and work in a clockwise spiral.

Answer 183

B. Based on the number alphabet backwards, add the values of the two letters on the outer edge of each segment and place the sum into the opposite segment on the inside.

Answer 184

− X + − ÷ +. $9 - 3 \times 4 + 19 - 8 \div 5 + 4 = 11$.

Answer 185

B. The others all have an equal number of straight lines and curves.

Answer 186

F. Circles and rectangles interchange except for strings of 3 circles which disappear.

Answer 187

Back, back, forward, back.

FINISH

START

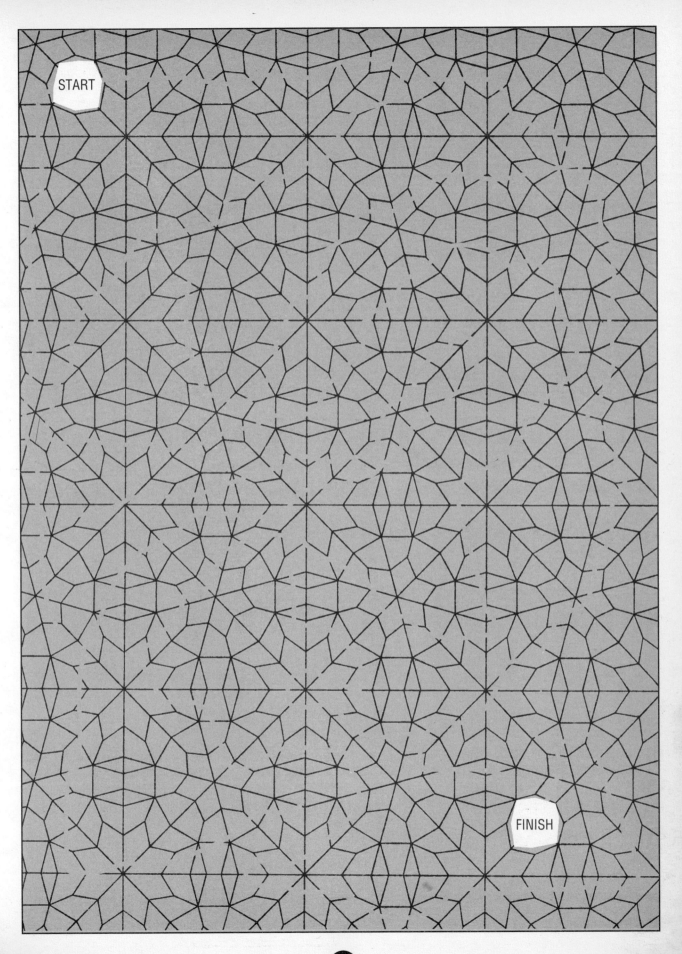

START

FINISH

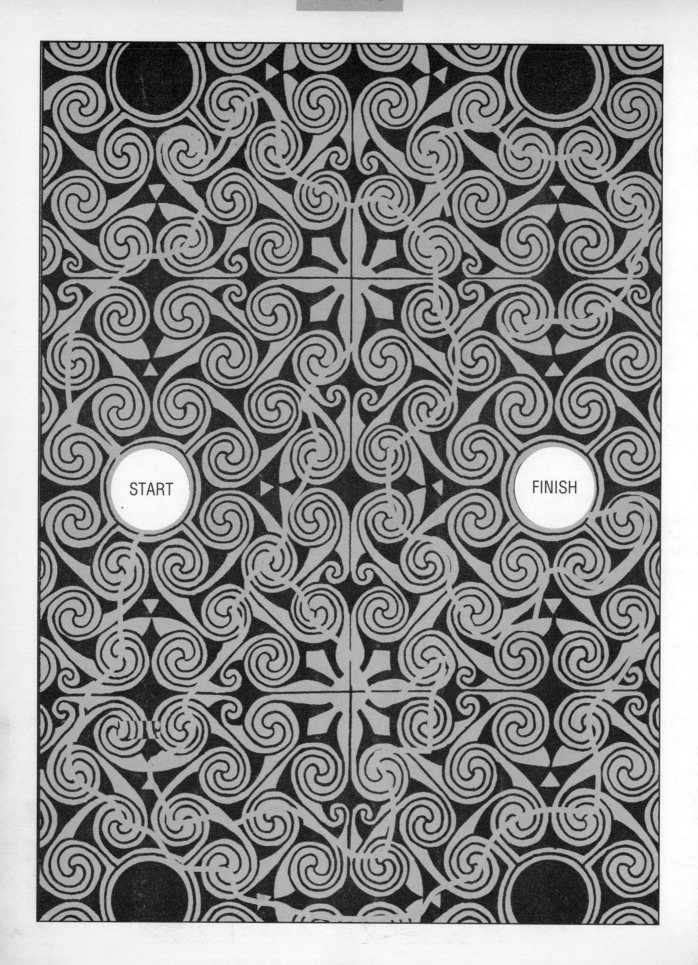

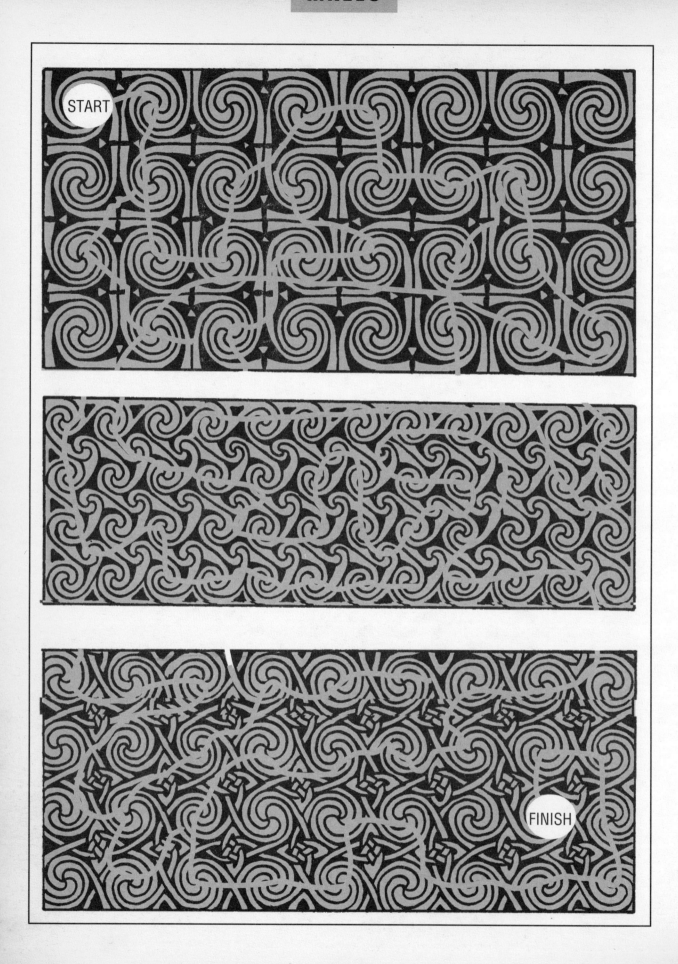

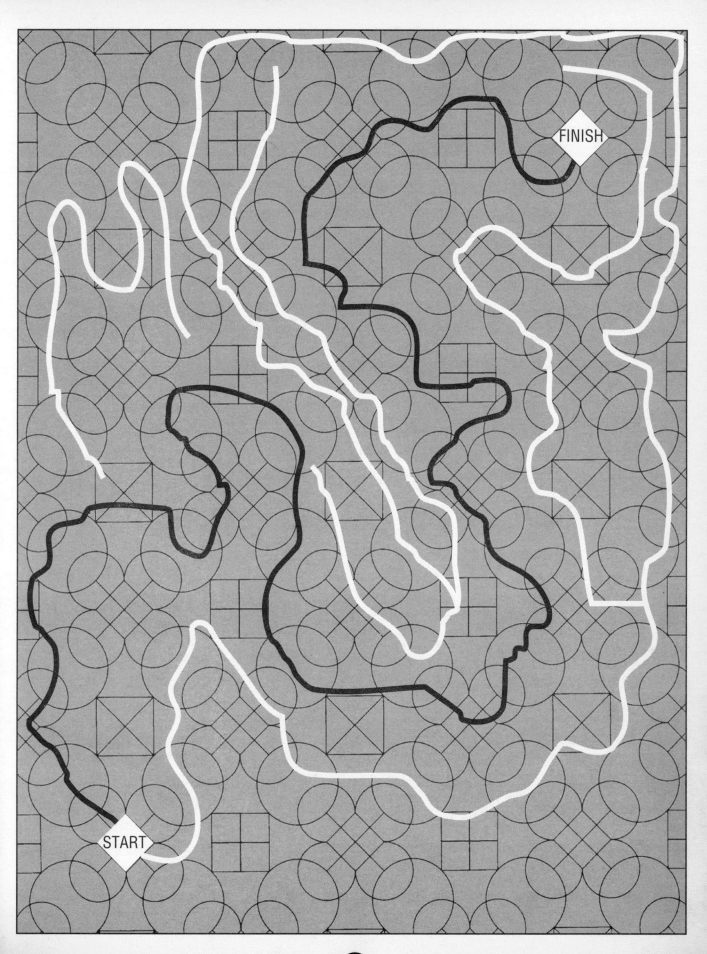

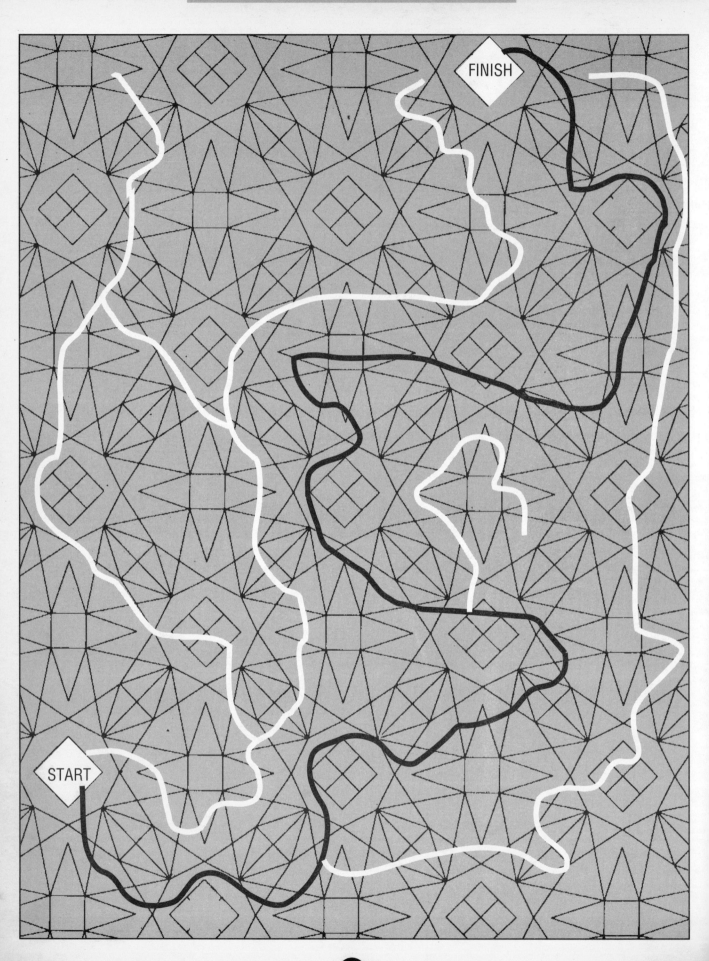

FINISH

START

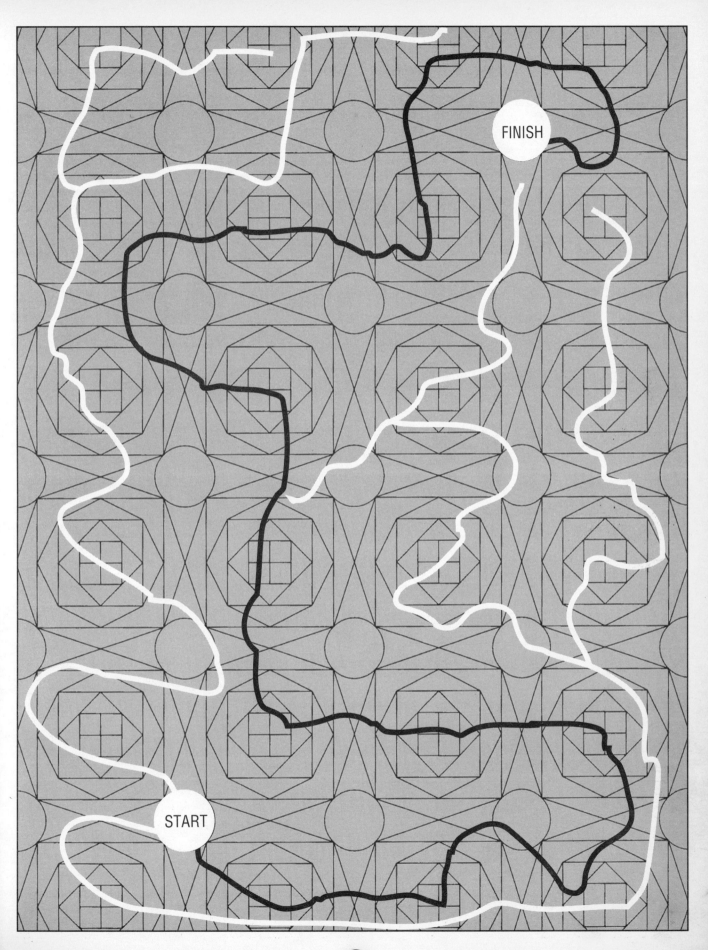

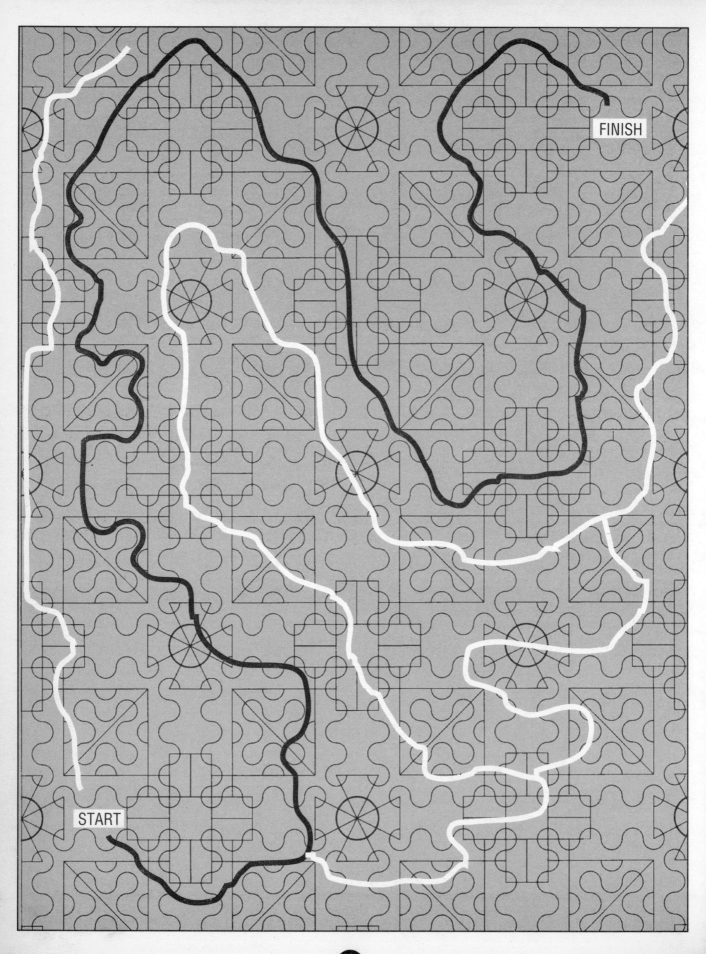

START

FINISH

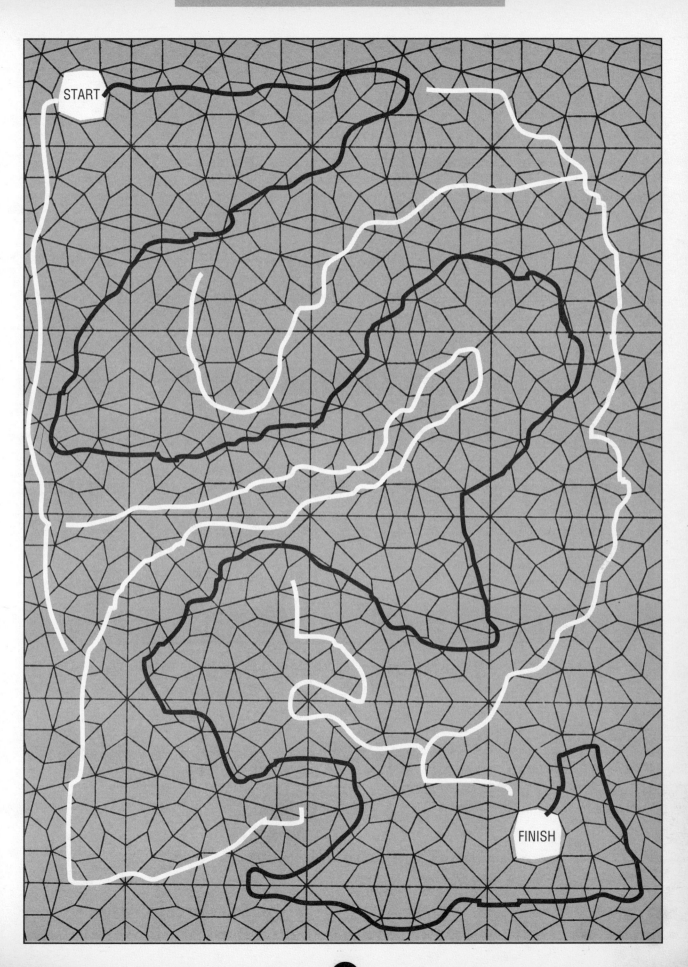

START

FINISH

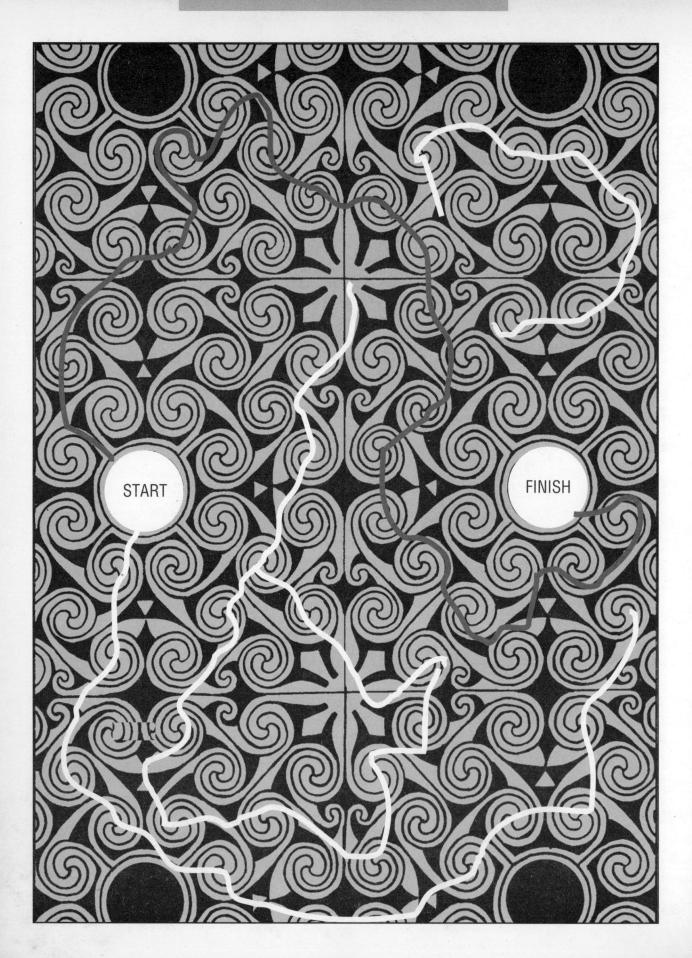

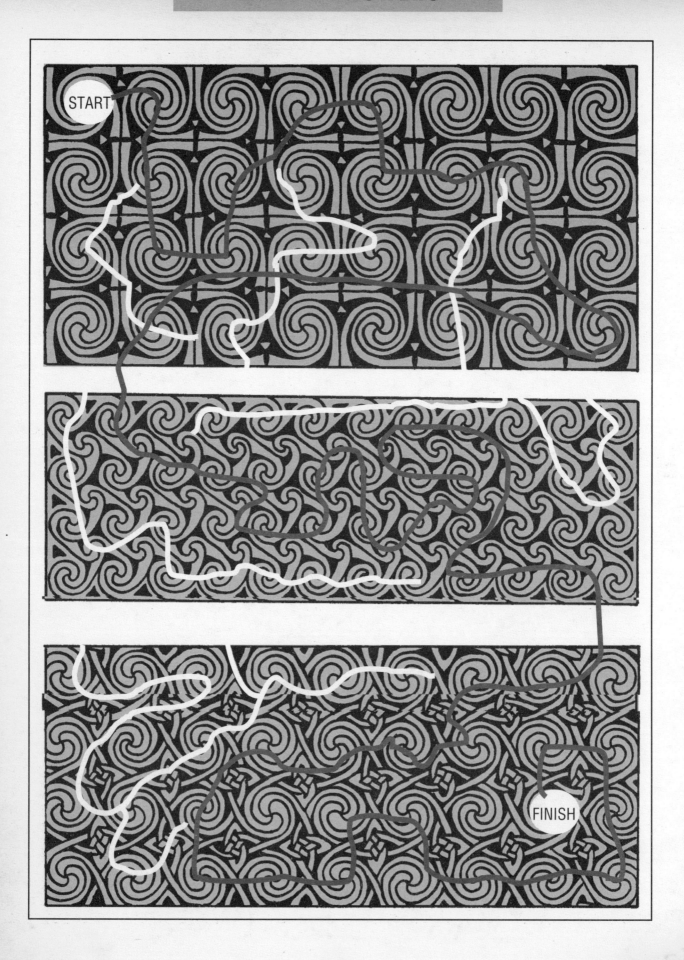

PUZZLE 1

Take a letter from each cloud in turn. You will find the surnames of five film actors plus one extra name. Who is it?

See answer 7

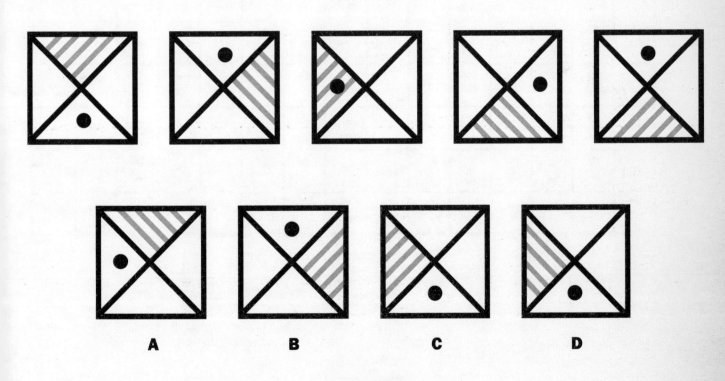

PUZZLE 2

Can you work out which symbol follows the series?

See answer 19

LEVEL 3

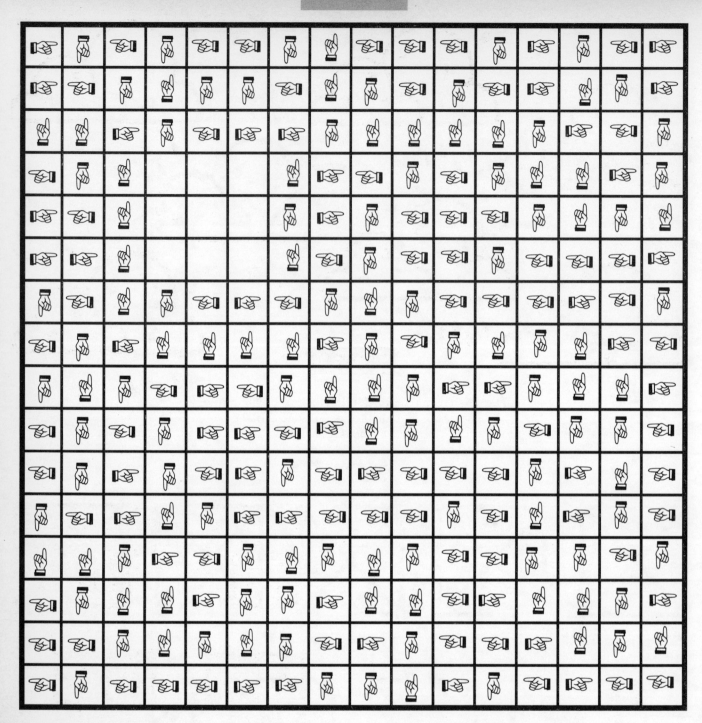

PUZZLE 3

Can you work out the reasoning behind this grid and complete the missing section?

See answer 11

PUZZLE 4

Take a letter from each cloud in the given order. You will find the names of five composers and one extra name. Who is it?

See answer 21

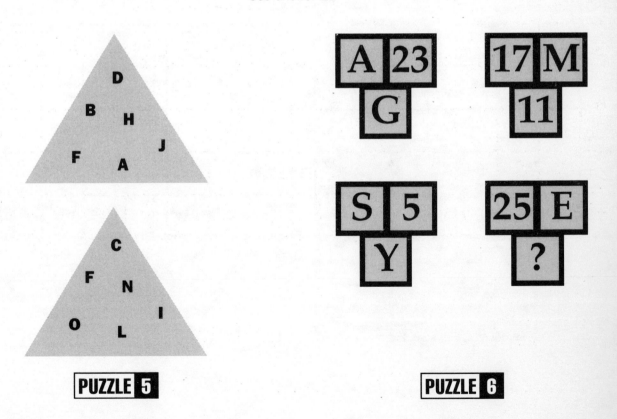

PUZZLE 5

Can you work out which are the two odd letters out in these triangles?

See answer 127

PUZZLE 6

Can you work out what should replace the question mark?

See answer 81

LEVEL 3

S4	E3	SW2	E8	E3	E3	SE3	SW1	SW6	S6	S1	W2
SE4	S2	SE5	S2	NE1	S6	SE3	SE4	W5	SW2	S1	W11
NE1	E5	N2	E2	W1	SE3	S1	W5	S4	E2	NE1	W4
NE2	S3	W2	N3	E6	NW1	NW2	W5	N1	E2	S3	W7
E2	SW1	NE4	SW1	S2	S2	W5	W1	W4	SE1	*	W1
E3	NE4	E7	SW2	E2	N2	SE2	N4	N1	N4	N5	S2
E6	N1	E9	NE2	NE1	NE3	NE1	NW6	W5	N4	W10	N2
NE3	N5	NE6	E4	W2	W2	E3	W1	W4	E1	NW3	W11

This diagram represents a treasure map. You are allowed stop on each square only once (though you may cross a square as often as you like). When you stop on a square you must follow the instructions you find there. The first one or two letters stand for points of the compass (N = North, S = South, etc.), the number for the number of steps you have to take. The finishing point is the square with the asterisk.
Can you find the starting point? There is one complication. You will find that you never land on some of the squares at all. If you cross out those squares on which you have landed you will see that those on which you have not fallen a two-figure number.
What is it?

See answer 14

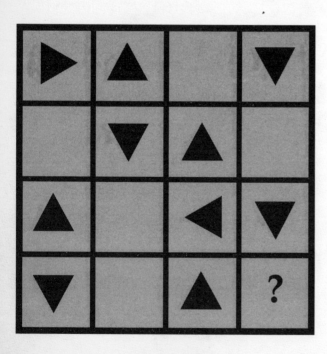

Can you work out the reasoning behind this diagram and fill in the last square?

See answer 5

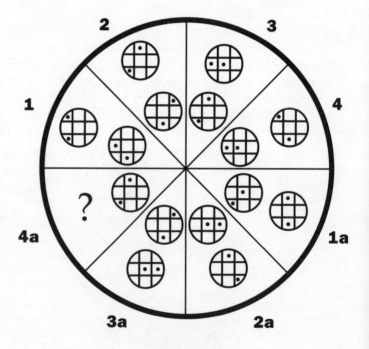

Can you work out what the missing symbol should look like?

See answer 1

PUZZLE 10

Joshua Shrimp had been at sea for forty years and in that time he had been right around the globe many times. **However, he had always spent his nights in bed and on dry land.**

How?

See answer 16

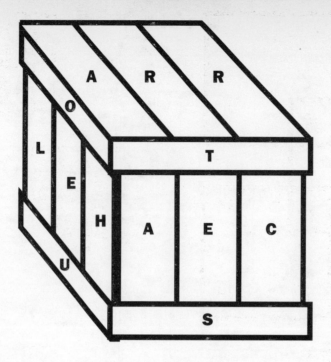

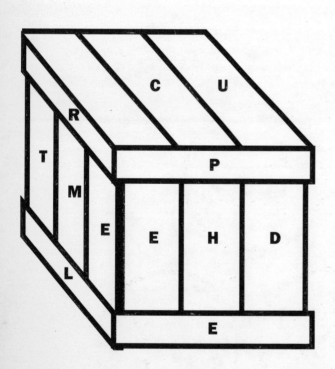

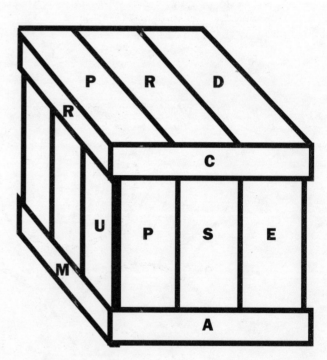

PUZZLE 11

These letters, when joined together correctly, make up a
novel and its author. Can you spot it?

See answer 22

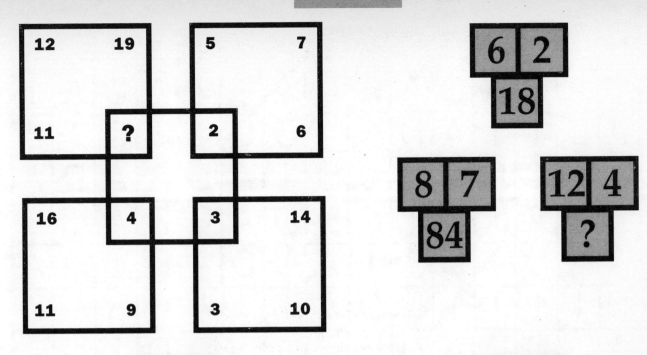

12	19
11	?

5	7
2	6

16	4
11	9

3	14
3	10

6	2
18	

8	7
84	

12	4
?	

PUZZLE 12

Can you find the number that should replace the question mark?

See answer 13

PUZZLE 13

Can you work out which number should replace the question mark?

See answer 20

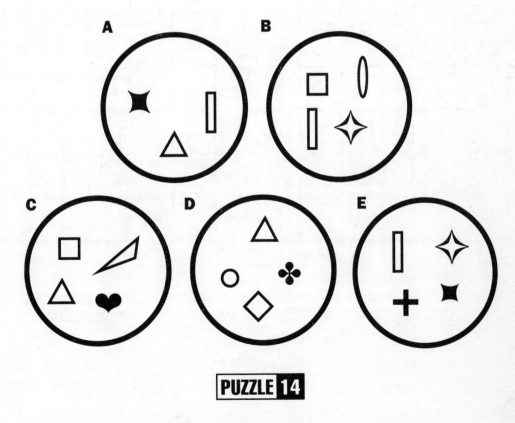

PUZZLE 14

Can you find the odd one out?

See answer 3

I	D	I	A	I	D	D	A	I	A	I	I	D	A	I	D
D	I	A	I	A	D	A	D	A	A	D	A	I	I	A	D
A	A	D	I	I	A	D	D	A	D	D	A	I	D	I	A
I	A	A	I	D	I	D	D	D	I	A	D	A	A	D	A
D	A	D	A	I	D	I	A	D	D	A	D	D	A	I	D
I	A	A	D	A	D	A	I	A	D	D	A	D	I	D	A
A	D	I	I	I	I	D	D	A	I	I	A	D	A	I	D
D	A	I	D	D	A	D	D	D	A	I	D	D	I	D	A
D	D	A	D	D	A	D	D	A	A	D	A	A	A	D	I
I	A	D	D	A	I	A	D	D	A	A	D	D	A	D	I
D	A	A	D	A	D	A	D	D	D	D	I	A	I	D	I
A	D	A	A	D	A	D	A	D	A	D	A	D	A	D	A
I	A	A	D	A	A	I	A	I	D	A	A	D	D	A	D
D	I	D	A	D	D	D	I	D	A	A	D	I	D	D	A
I	D	A	D	D	D	A	A	I	D	I	D	A	A	I	A
A	I	A	D	A	A	D	I	D	A	D	I	I	D	I	D

PUZZLE 15

In this grid the word AIDA, written without a change of direction, appears only once. It can be written forwards and backwards in a horizontal, vertical or diagonal direction. Can you spot it?

See answer 10

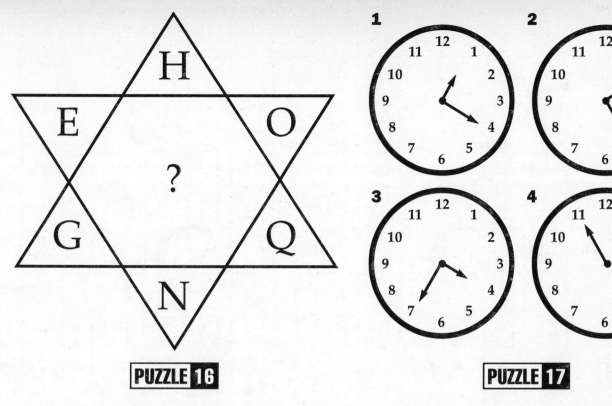

PUZZLE 16

Can you unravel the reasoning behind this star and fill in the missing letter?

See answer 17

PUZZLE 17

Can you work out what number the missing hour hand on clock 4 should point at?

See answer 24

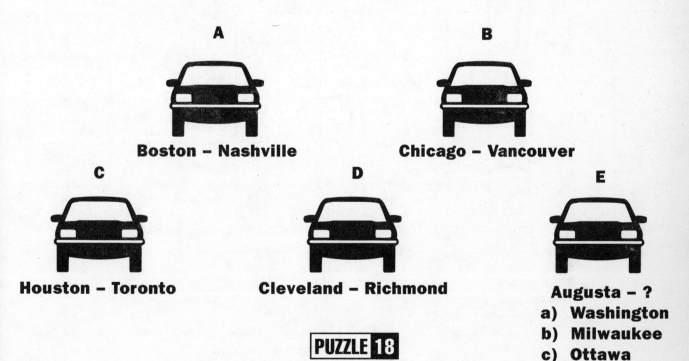

A Boston – Nashville

B Chicago – Vancouver

C Houston – Toronto

D Cleveland – Richmond

E Augusta – ?
a) Washington
b) Milwaukee
c) Ottawa
d) Galveston

PUZZLE 18

Can you unravel the logic behind the starting point and destination of each of these cars and find out where car E is going?

See answer 4

PUZZLE 19

Pick one letter from each flower in the order shown. You will get the names of five statesmen. Who are they?

See answer 8

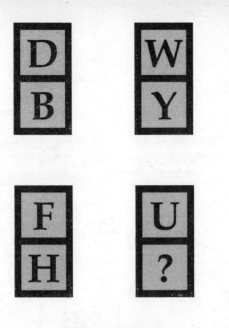

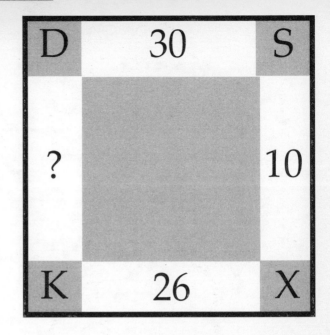

PUZZLE 20

Can you unravel the reasoning behind these domino pieces and find the missing letter?

See answer 23

PUZZLE 21

Can you work out which number should replace the question mark?

See answer 15

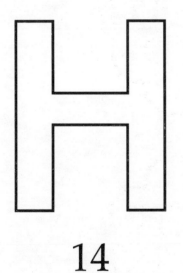  

14 ? 29

PUZZLE 22

Can you work out which number fits underneath letter A?

See answer 6

		2	7	3	8	4	9		2	7	3	8	4	9
9	9								2	7	3	8	4	9
4	4	3	8	4	9									
8	8	7			2	7	3	8	4	9				
3	3	2		4	9									
7	7			8	7	3	8	4	9				2	
2	2			3	2								7	
				7									3	
				2									8	2
													4	7
9													9	3
4														8
8					9	4	8	3	7	2				4
3					9	4	8	3	7	2				9
7		9	4	8	3	7	2							
2					9	4	8	3	7	2				

PUZZLE 23

The numbers in this grid occur in the following order:
9, 4, 8, 3, 7, 2 and run in an anti-clockwise spiral
starting at the top right. It is complicated by the addition
of spaces and repeats according to a pattern.
Can you complete the missing section?

See answer 9

Bill and his brother, Tom, were at the airport seeing their elderly mother off on holiday.

Suddenly Bill saw a man in the crowd.

"Here, Tom, do you see who that is?"

"I don't believe it!", gasped Tom. "It's Phil!"

He was quite right. But how did they both recognize Phil?

Neither brother had ever seen him before.

See answer 12

Answer 1
Reading across segments 1 and 1a, 2 and 2a, etc. the dots move around the circle in a vertical boustrophedon.

Answer 2
A and **N**. The series is B, D, F, H, J (2, 4, 6, 8, 10). Add 1, 2, 3, 4, 5 respectively to the values to get the letters in the second triangle.

Answer 3
C. It is the only circle with an asymmetrical shape.

Answer 4
D. Take the values of the first two letters of each starting town, the first based on the alphabet forward (A = 1, Z = 26) and the second on the alphabet backward (A = 26, Z = 1). Add the values together. The new letter of that value will be the first letter of the new town.

Answer 5
Start at the top right and move across the square in a horizontal boustrophedon. The pattern is: miss 1 square, turn by 180°, turn by 90° clockwise, miss 1, turn by 90° clockwise, turn by 180°.

Answer 6
6. Divide the number of sides of the letter by 2 and add the value of the letter, based on its position in the alphabet.

Answer 7
Costner, Cushing, Dunaway, Garland, Hepburn. The extra one is Domingo.

Answer 8
Brezhnev, Disraeli, Thatcher, Adenauer, Pompidou.

Answer 9

		2
9		7
4	8	3

I	D	I	A	I	D	D	A	I	A	I	I	D	A	I	D
D	I	A	I	A	D	A	A	D	A	I	I	A	D	A	I
A	A	D	I	I	A	D	D	A	D	D	A	I	D	I	A
I	A	A	I	D	I	D	D	D	I	A	D	A	A	D	A
D	A	D	A	I	D	I	A	D	D	A	D	D	A	I	D
I	A	A	D	A	D	A	I	A	D	D	A	D	I	D	A
A	D	I	A	I	I	D	D	A	I	I	A	D	A	I	D
D	A	I	D	D	A	D	D	D	A	I	D	D	I	D	D
D	A	D	A	D	D	A	D	D	A	A	D	A	A	D	I
I	A	D	D	A	I	A	D	D	A	A	D	D	A	D	I
D	A	A	D	A	D	A	D	D	D	D	I	A	I	D	I
A	D	A	A	D	A	D	A	D	A	D	A	D	A	D	A
I	A	A	D	A	A	I	A	I	D	A	A	D	D	A	D
D	I	D	A	D	D	D	I	D	A	A	D	I	D	D	A
I	D	A	D	D	D	A	A	I	D	I	D	A	A	I	A
A	I	A	D	A	A	D	I	D	A	D	I	I	D	I	D

Answer 10

223

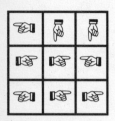

Answer 11
The pattern sequence is shown below. Starting at the bottom right, work in a diagonal boustrophedon (clockwise start).

Answer 12
Their mother had produced triplets. However, being poor she had been unable to bring them all up and had given one up for adoption. Nevertheless, the family resemblance was so strong that the men recognized their long lost brother.

Answer 13
7. Add the three numbers on the outside of each square (A). Add the digits of the sum (B). Divide A by B and place in the small square.

Answer 14
The starting point is at Row 1, Col 1. The number is 31. Start at the finishing point and work back.

Answer 15
38. Regard the alphabet as a circle. The number is double the number of spaces between the letters.

Answer 16
He was captain of a river boat ferry. The globe he went round was a decorative one he had in his cabin.

Answer 17
K. K is the same number of spaces in the alphabet from H and N, O and G, and E and Q.

Answer 18
19. Write the alphabet in a circle. The numbers represent values of letters based on the alphabet backwards (A = 26, Z = 1). Start at A, miss 2, D (=23), miss 2, G, etc.

Answer 19
D. The striped section moves clockwise by 1, 2, 3 and 4 sections (repeat). Each time it moves by 2 and 4 sections the pattern is reflected. The dot moves 2 sections clockwise and 1 section anti-clockwise alternately.

Answer 20
72. Halve the number on the top left, multiply the number on the top right by 3. Multiply the two resulting numbers with each other, and put the product in the bottom square.

Answer 21
Rossini, Puccini, Debussy, Berlioz, Corelli. The extra one is Cezanne.

Answer 22
A la Recherche du Temps Perdu by Marcel Proust.

Answer 23
S. D is the 4th letter from the start of the alphabet, W is the 4th from the end. F is the 6th from the start, U the 6th from the end, etc.

Answer 24
8. The two numbers added together give the number the minute hand points at on the next clock. The hour hand points at the number three spaces before.